HARRIS

YOUR NO-BS PRACTICAL STEP BY STEP GUIDE
TO FINALLY BECOME RICH AND FREE

RULES

TIM & JULIE HARRIS

This book is dedicated:

To all of you who think you are alone without direction.
To all of you who are looking for truth.
To all of those who truly desire to be rich and free.
To all of those who know that their path forward
is being of service to others.
This book is for you.

"Before enlightenment, chop wood, carry water...After enlightenment, chop wood, carry water."

- Zen Proverb

Other books by Tim and Julie Harris

The Real Estate Treasure Map

Think & Grow Rich for Real Estate

90 Day Massive Action Plan

25 Sure-Fire Lead Generators

Price Reductions: The Bottom Dollar
Script for a Guaranteed Sale

Published by Best Seller Publishing®, Pasadena, CA
Best Seller Publishing® is a registered trademark
Printed in the United States of America.
ISBN 978-1-946978-25-7

This publication is designed to provide accurate and authoritative information with regard to the subject matter covered. It is sold with the understanding that the publisher is not engaged in rendering legal, accounting, or other professional advice. If legal advice or other expert assistance is required, the services of a competent professional should be sought. The opinions expressed by the authors in this book are not endorsed by Best Seller Publishing® and are the sole responsibility of the author rendering the opinion.

Most Best Seller Publishing® titles are available at special quantity discounts for bulk purchases for sales promotions, premiums, fundraising, and educational use. Special versions or book excerpts can also be created to fit specific needs.

For more information, please write:
Best Seller Publishing®
1346 Walnut Street, #205
Pasadena, CA 91106
or call 1(626) 765 9750
Toll Free: 1(844) 850-3500
Visit us online at: www.BestSellerPublishing.org

Table of Contents

Introduction

Why are we writing this book? Because we know, firsthand, the frustration that those who are trying to establish a career in the field of real estate often feel. Being a real estate professional is neither as easy or glamorous as it is frequently portrayed by some cable television shows. Having said that, for those who are willing to put forth the necessary effort to meet challenges head-on, and are willing to commit the necessary time, a career in real estate can be personally satisfying and lucrative. It is frequently said that there is no substitute for hard work and we're not here to disagree with that. Experience is a great teacher and it's our aim to help you avoid mistakes, and provide you with an organizational system to help you create a supportive team to implement your ideas to establish and run your business.

I want to share a simple story that always pops to mind when I'm speaking with various agents and brokers. When my husband, Tim, and I were freshly licensed and just beginning our careers in real estate, we didn't even know what we didn't know — about anything. We had just started with Re/Max because it looked like a good location and more importantly, it was near our tiny starter home. This was in the days prior to the Internet and our broker sat us down and gave us a Re/Max catalog of stuff to buy. The question was: Where should we start? What should we invest in? How should we market ourselves? How should we generate leads? What should we do to follow up? These questions and a thousand others were on our mind. We thumbed through this huge catalog of stuff we were supposed to be spending money on with no real idea how to make choices, just as today agents are attacked every morning, noon and night with email and text offers, promising to be the best thing ever for their business.

Where does business come from? Everyone wants to believe in an easy button, a silver bullet or some secret. If I just do this, everything will be great. We believe in teaching the multi-spoke model, which we'll get into in the book. Our view is that there's not just one solution; you must be doing several different things. Because there's not a lot of specific and obvious direction, whether you're a new agent or you're a grizzled veteran, or you're getting back to the business, we want to address that, and help every agent and broker who are ready to listen. This book is designed to give you the specific, proven rules of engagement that you can count on to serve you well in your pursuit of your real-estate funded goals and dreams.

In the beginning, generating leads was our job #1. Then as we progressed, and as our skill developed, there arose a second question: What should we do next? Everywhere you look, someone is telling you something different. Follow me. Follow this system. Follow that plan. Invest in this online lead-generation. We felt we were being pulled many different directions at once. Lots of *try this*, and *try that*, versus *follow these rules and you win*.

Through our coaching experience, we hear every day that this continues to be a problem. What do I do? I have no direction. I have no business plan. There is a huge lack of leadership and direction in this industry so that you cannot only be successful, but also have longevity, while maintaining a fulfilling lifestyle.

In our first full year in real estate, we sold over 100 homes and were fortunate to continue that record for the ensuing decade. During that period, we noticed the questions that concerned us initially had changed. Now the focus was how to *keep* our income. How to not spend every dollar so we could continue to increase our income. Questions arose, like whether to have a team and if so, should it be big or small? Or should we have no team at all? Later still, the question was whether to choose to go up market. If you've figured out how many listings you need, your "magic number," how do you decide what you're going to go after? Should you go after more expensive inventory? Should you change markets? Should you move? The questions change as you become more experienced. This book is here to clarify some very specific rules of engagement, which will serve agents well in navigating their way to success, whether you just got your license yesterday, or whether you're looking at an exit plan, or you're somewhere in between.

We called this book *Harris Rules* because we figured out these rules along our career and through many hundreds of thousands of coaching calls. If you have specific rules to follow and an exact plan, it's going to get you from Point A to Point B faster, with less stress and fewer questions and confusion along the road. Questions in real estate cost time and money. We're here to lay down the groundwork, and to give you real world, practical, ethical, authentic leadership in an industry that often has either no leadership or leadership with ulterior motives. This is the greatest opportunity for a motivated person to make a difference in the lives of others, through providing great service, as well as creating personal wealth, which results from doing great work. If you're not yet making all of the money that you need to make in this practice, it's usually due to one simple fact — you haven't figured out how to help enough people, at a high enough level, with enough consistency, to create that wealth so that you can then continue to contribute.

This book offers specific rules to answer those questions. We're going to cover mindset, which is how you need to think about the business. Then we'll cover an action plan, which is what you need to do not just to make money, but to have longevity and to create the life of your dreams. Next, we'll cover how to decide to scale the business and how to continue to monetize it. We're going to start from the beginning, because if the mindset isn't there, then the rest doesn't matter. Mindset is how you need to think, the action plan is what you need to do, and scaling is how to monetize.

CHAPTER 1

Mindset and Motivation

RULE #1: I'm a Doer. I Do Things Now. I Get Things Done.

Motivation is the linchpin of a successful career in real estate. The first aspect of motivation consists of mindset, so let's define it. Mindset is a fixed mental attitude or disposition that predetermines a person's responses to and interpretations of situations. It also can simply be an inclination or a habit. Our part one is all about motivation. Let's get a greater understanding of it.

Motivation is simply what drives you to achieve the things that are important to you. Daniel Goleman, author of several books on emotional intelligence, has identified four elements that make up motivation: personal drive to achieve; the desire to improve or to meet certain standards and then to commit to personal or organizational goals; initiative, which he defines as "readiness to act on opportunities"; and optimism, the ability to keep going and pursue goals in the face of setbacks.

Motivation affects your mindset, your attitude, on an hourly, if not minute-by-minute, basis. Your actions are based on your level of motivation, or possibly your lack thereof. We hear during coaching calls time and time again that no one is highly motivated 100 per cent of the time. It's a myth that you're either motivated or you're not; that's just not true. You may be super motivated at certain times of day or days of the week. Other times, you might not feel like getting out of bed. That's the human condition. It's reality, but it's also something that you can absolutely modify and manipulate. There's nothing wrong with you if you don't feel motivated all the time about everything. There may be something wrong with you if you don't recognize the control you have to choose how motivated you feel in different situations.

The rule however, must be to control your mindset. Accept that this is not possible 100% of the time, but also accept that without the attempt to control your own mindset, something or someone else will always direct you how to feel and think, and may easily be able to manipulate you.

Here's a mindset action step. Make the decision to understand your personal motivation and to take control of it. An example of your amazing, but possibly underutilized, ability to control your motivation, not to mention your efficiency, is how you feel right before a vacation. In the time prior to taking a vacation, you're super organized. You edit the things on your to-do list to only the most necessary. You're awesome at managing your time and getting things done. It's almost miraculous how efficient you become.

David Allen, one of my favorite authors, writes in *Getting Things Done: The Art of Stress-Free Productivity*, "Most people feel best about their work the week before their vacation, but it's not because of the vacation itself. What do you do the last week, (and as a coach I would say even the last day) before you leave on a big trip? Well, what do you do? Well, you clean up. You close up. You clarify. You renegotiate all your agreements with yourself and others. I suggest that you do this weekly instead of yearly."

As a coach, I suggest that it behooves you to look at this daily. What would happen if you treated each workday as if you had that plane to catch for your vacation? What would that do to your motivation? The next time you're having trouble getting motivated and moving, repeat our rule: I'm a doer. I do things now. I get things done!"

Next, we want to look at internal versus external motivations. This is a huge "aha" moment for most of our coaching clients. This is one of the fundamental differences between agents who "get it" and get to the next level, versus agents who struggle from check to check, from deal to deal, and have maybe only a handful of deals at a time.

Let's examine internal versus external motivation. Have you wondered why somehow you can always make your car payment, your mobile phone payment, especially in real estate, and your house or rent payment? All of those things, somehow, get paid. Maybe even via automatic draft. Those are all examples of external motivation. Something bad happens to you if you don't comply with that obligation. Your cell gets turned off if you don't pay your Verizon bill, for example. Cell phone companies don't mess around and you knew the deal when you signed that contract. That's external motivation. Their rule is, "if you pay, you stay; if you don't, you won't." It's pretty simple.

Why is it that something like building up your nest egg, so that you have at least a year of reserves, or losing that 20 pounds, or buying two new rental properties, or traveling to Paris, just keeps getting put off? Why does one procrastinate on those types of activities? Those things are a lot more exciting than paying your cell phone bill, wouldn't you agree? It's because this is internal motivation, which curiously, is weaker than external motivation. When nothing immediate happens to you, and there is no immediate negative consequence if you don't do something, it becomes much easier to procrastinate. Thus, you need Rule #1, help with controlling your mindset. Control your procrastination thoughts.

Set into motion the actions necessary to achieve the things you currently claim are important, yet keep being put off.

After years of coaching agents and other business people, one thing we've learned is that you must bridge the gap in your thinking. You must learn to take your personal, internal motivation as seriously as if it were the external kind. This is a mindset leap.

Though this applies to all non-external goals, the easiest and most salient example is to look at your finances. Here's a fact: the difference between top producers and the rest is that top producers take their personal goals as seriously as they do their external obligations. In our organization, you're a top producer if you have well-thought-out, specific goals and you're meeting or exceeding them, or at least working hard to get there. That's a top producer to us. The difference between those top producers and everyone else is quite specific.

They are in better control of their mindset.

It's a fact that top agents always know two numbers off the top of their head. They know what it takes for them to live on, to pay their bills, and to keep the lights on, and clothing on their children. They also know the income necessary to meet the needs of leading the life of their dreams. Most people, when put on the spot and asked, "How much money would it take for you to lead the life of your dreams," will say, "Millions." Or they'll say, "At least a million more." That's if they have an answer at all. Many of them don't. Many of them just say, "I need to do more. I need to be doing better." Those are not real answers. "More" and "better" are not concrete numbers. Harris Rules require that you know those two numbers at all times.

Top producers, because they follow the rule of controlling one's mindset, know that any day they haven't generated money to first "run them," and then go above and beyond, that they're actually falling behind.

The difference between where you are now and where you need to be to feel a significant improvement in lifestyle, including paying off debt, buying an awesome house, building up huge reserves, and having the freedom to travel, is less than you think. We know that for most agents, based on our countless coaching calls and years of experience, the difference is really about a 3:1 ratio. In other words, for you to make that leap in lifestyle, it takes about three times what you're currently averaging in commissions earned monthly, and doing it consistently month in and month out. So, there are actually two leaps you've got to make after you realize what your numbers are.

The freedom comes from knowing these numbers so that you can then act to do something about it. Not knowing keeps you simply paying your bills on time and fantasizing about what could be if you just did "more" — that nebulous number. Or more commonly, by convincing yourself that your lifestyle won't change unless you make at least a million dollars more, which is probably not even necessary.

In our observation, a typical agent must make about $5,000 per month to meet his or her financial obligations. You can adjust that for the size of family. We have coaching clients who have eight kids all in private schools. Obviously, their costs are going to be more. Also, adjustments may be made for differences in marketplace. If you're only making $5,000 per month and you live in Manhattan, well, you're below the poverty line. By and large, let's just use this as an easy example. Most agents must make about $5,000 per month to meet their financial obligations.

That same agent could pay off his debt, save a nice nest egg, take two or three awesome vacations a year, and upgrade his house, car, and wardrobe, for about $15,000 per month. Again, here's a secondary leap of faith: You've got to do this month in and month out.

Let's do some math.

Use this Knowing Your Numbers formula to know what you REALLY need to earn to achieve your personal, business, family, and financial goals this year!

Monthly

A. Personal Overhead $_____ B. Business Overhead $_____ C. "Fun": This is the money necessary for you to accomplish all of your "fun" goals this year. If you skip this category, you won't have any fun! If it's not planned for, it doesn't happen. $_____ D. Taxes: Add up A, B, and C, and add 25% as a general rule of thumb. Some people pay more, some less, but 25% will allow you to prepare for taxes. $_____ E. Savings: All real estate agents say, "I want to save more"; decide how much more. A good place to start is at least 90 days of personal and business savings. If you already have that, work on having one year of reserves saved. $_____.

B. Add up A + B + C + D + E = Income required to earn per MONTH = $_____ My outside income is: $_____ (This is any non-real estate income, including spouse's income, investment income, etc.) The difference is: (take income required from above, and subtract outside income.) = $_____. It's okay if you don't have any outside income. Many agents don't. But if you do have money coming in from somewhere else, if it's predictable income, you need to account for it. What I MUST EARN: $_____ / Month.

Take the amount from What I MUST EARN, and multiply it by twelve to equal your required YEARLY income for personal, business, savings, taxes, and fun. That amount is: $_____. You will need this figure later, when you use the Income and Unit Calculator, which shows you how you're going to accomplish this income.

Would you like a FREE copy of Tim and Julie's proven business plan?
http://FreeCoachingCallsForAgents.com

Part Two: The amount of my average net commission is: $_____

Secret: If you're not sure, ask your broker if he or she tracked this for you. If you're a NEW agent, find out the average sale price in your area and use the average net commission based on that price.

Secret: Net commission is what you KEEP after all broker splits, any processing fees, etc. Take the amount you must earn per MONTH and divide by your average net commission. This will reveal the number of transactions necessary to cover your personal, business, savings, fun, and tax requirements each month. Amount needed per month, divided by my average net commission = _____ deals needed monthly, x 12 = deals necessary yearly.

Part Three: I am currently averaging _____ deals per month. This does/does not cover my personal, business, savings, taxes, and fun. (Circle your answer.) I am/am not satisfied with continuing to earn at this level. (Circle your answer.)

Secret: If you keep doing what you've been doing, you'll keep producing what you've been producing — or — you'll slide backward as other agents, who have upgraded their skills, education, mindset, and goal setting, pass you by. Don't let this happen to you!

Am I motivated by fear? Am I motivated by incentive? What is driving me? We will examine these questions more in our goal setting modules. After completing the exercise above, you know how much you must earn monthly and how many deals are required for you to produce. Don't worry if it's more or less than you thought. Keep working through this business plan so you will have the confidence and the know-how required to create your Real Estate Treasure – the amount required to achieve your personal, business, savings, and fun objectives, and also to pay your taxes.

After we complete the math from that section, we conclude with one thought: *freedom.* That's why you got into real estate. Freedom, in this respect, does have a number attached to it. It's your new monthly commitment. You must think of it in the same way you did your old core monthly overhead and make the mental leap to embrace the new reality. You will implement things necessary to get to the next level.

In fact, your subconscious mind is already at work putting this all together. I can guarantee that in the next 20 minutes, you will write down two or three leads that you had previously forgotten, because of this new higher focus and changed mindset you now have. You'll find that your ability to, as Tim Harris says, "Do what you don't want to do when you don't want to do it" at the highest level comes to you more easily and more frequently.

It's time to start thinking about your fantasy number, which will accomplish all of your goals (we're going to do goal setting in the next section) as seriously as you take your cell phone bill, your mortgage or your rent payment, and your car payment; those things that would have a serious, negative effect you if you didn't pay them. You've got to take what you **want to do** as seriously as what you **have to do.**

The practical application requires: first, accurately completing the Knowing Your Numbers exercise; and second, memorizing your core financial commitment number. That's what it takes for you to keep the lights on, and your new, fantasy financial commitment number. Be sure to express this in *monthly* income figures. You can come back to this after you work on the next section, which will help you polish those goals. Finally, compare your current average net commissions and units versus what it will take for you to achieve your next level.

Typically, we see an agent who has figured out how to average three transactions per month, providing him with enough to live, but not enough to live his fantasy lifestyle. He makes his mortgage, pays his bills and keeps the lights on. Typically, he'll need to bump up his transactions per month, from his usual average of three, to maybe four or five per month to achieve a significant difference in lifestyle and goals.

The following is a real-life case study that plays into all of this. We gave you a financial example, but some of you may still be hung up. "Well, how can I do that if I don't have passion about real estate?" I used to feel like I couldn't find motivation to be great at real estate because, by training, I am a classical musician, a completely, utterly unrelated profession. Music was my passion. Real estate never felt natural. I wasn't a born salesperson.

That changed when I went to a Howard Brinton event in 1997 and went to a superstar talent show. I thought it would be a joke. A superstar talent show for realtors? Really? What could realtors possibly have to offer in the way of talent? That was my arrogant, classical musician ego speaking.

I was amazed to see incredible talent acts that were in no way remotely related to real estate. Russell Shaw did a side-splitting standup comedy act. Gary Ubaldini sang and accompanied himself on guitar. He was crazy talented. You never would have guessed it, but both Russ and Gary were, and still are, extremely successful realtors.

At that point, on that day, I realized that I didn't have to have passion for real estate. I recognized that I could find passion for the freedom that real estate could afford me. I've had many coaching calls with agents like you who feel the same way. You're artists. You're musicians. You're talented in sports. You have other passions. Real estate has just been paying your bills, but you've become stuck there.

At this point in my life, I've played on a soundtrack, and performed with the Pacific Symphony. I consider that I have been successful in music. Now, I would say my success has at least, partially, been due to real estate. I've met friends in music who were dependent upon music to make only an okay living. They lost their passion for it. I get to have my cake and eat it, too.

Eventually, I realized that there was a cost to that freedom, the freedom to pursue what my passion is. That cost was identified by a specific income that paid our overhead, kept taxes caught up, socked money into savings, and accounted for travel and fun items. Only then did the pursuit of my passion become more fun. The pressure to make money in music was gone, thus the ability to make money in real estate was unleashed. This was the price tag for my personal freedom.

How do you apply these points to your lives? Motivation comes from getting in touch with why you're in this business. As coaches, we hear lots of answers to this question. Those answers include: You're in real estate so you can be your own boss, manage your own time, not have an income cap, live wherever you want to, be accountable to only yourself, earn more money, pay for your kids' or grandkids' education, pay off debt, get a better house, car, boat, vacation home, finally, have some savings, and shorten the path to retirement. Some of you answered this question with: recover from the recession causing me to sell all of my rentals, rebuild wealth after the Great Recession, or other wealth-crushing events, buy some rental properties, and do some flips.

Guess what? It all boils down to one simple word: freedom. All the things I rattled off are true, but at the end of the day, it's freedom.

What does freedom mean to me and my family?

When I have been the most motivated in the past, it was because I

_____

_____.

Three people I know who are more motivated than I am are: _____

_____

_____.

What makes them tick? _____
_____.

What I can implement today to manage my motivation ebbs and flows? _____
_____.

What works for me? _____
_____.

What do I need to stop doing? _____
_____.

What do I need to start doing? _____
_____.

What do I have to do when I don't want to do it at the highest level? _____
_____.

What or who do I need to get help from to get serious about it? __
_____
_____.

Practical, Tactical, Exercise: How Much Does It Cost to "Run You?"

Everyone has a daily cost of living, just because you're breathing, eating, driving and using electricity. That's just to exist, not to get ahead.

Cost of your monthly have-to-pay bills:

Rent or mortgage: $

Car payment or payments: $

Health insurance: $

Auto insurance: $

Grocery bill: $

Credit card minimum payments: $

Student loans: $

Utilities: $

Mobile phone: $

Cable / Internet: $

Other: $

Total: $_____ divide by 30 days in the month = $___daily burn rate_____

In other words, it takes $_____ per day to "run you" (and your family).

CHAPTER 2

Goal Setting

RULE #2: Have S.M.A.R.T Goals

A goal is a dream with an action plan. It's worth repeating: A goal is a dream with an action plan. There is a big difference between what a goal is and what a dream is. A dream that we hear at real estate seminars all the time is, "I'd like to make more money." By the way, I've never heard anybody say, "I want to make less money." A dream is essentially a wish: "I'd like to make more money" or "I'd like to lose weight." How many times do you hear those wishes? Well, what's the difference between a wish and a goal? A goal sounds like this: "I need to make three times what I'm making now so I can pay off my credit cards, pay cash for a new car, have one year of savings in reserves, cover my monthly overhead, and keep current with my taxes. I will accomplish this by doing A, B, and C and I'll do it by this date."

Do you see that there is a difference? We can think of goals by the acronym SMART. It stands for: specific, measurable, attainable, realistic, and timely. Instead of saying, "I'd like to make more money," put a dollar amount on it. What's more money? Is "more" a dollar, or is "more" a million dollars? What would it take to actually pay off your credit cards, pay cash for a new car, have a year of reserves, cover your monthly overhead, and keep your taxes current? That is a number that defines "more" for you.

Okay, so you may already be feeling some resistance at this point to goal setting. If you're like many of our coaching clients, mentally, you may be saying to yourself, "Well, I've never been a goal setter. What if I fall short? What if I fail?" To address those concerns, we always like to use the "shooting the arrow" example.

Even if you've never shot a bow and arrow before, you can visualize facing a target. When you shoot at the bullseye, do you aim below it, at it, or above it? Well, most people know that you need to aim above the goal if you intend to hit the bullseye. Goals are exactly like that. It's okay if you fall a little short of the center circle; you're still in the ring. You still have the goal of shooting that arrow at a specific objective, but by and large, shooting over it will get you where you need to go. That's okay, don't be too obsessed about hitting it exactly.

Although, as you'll see as we get further into the book, one needs to be careful what is wished for, because the way we teach goals is extremely effective. Maybe you are saying, "I'm afraid of accountability, I don't know what it looks like to achieve that." This brings up another key point that we often see as coaches. Some of you have lack of exposure to people who are achieving and living at a higher level. One of the things that we ask when someone is not sure what their goals should be, aside from the easy ones like paying off debt and paying off a tax bill, for instance, or something else that's quite tangible, "Well, where do you go from there?"

How do you set goals? You start by identifying people who are living more successfully than you. Maybe you don't know people who are more successful than you. You just don't know what success looks like. You don't know what your goal should be. Typically, we'll send you to the magazine section at Barnes and Noble and say, "Why don't you pick out 10 magazines that you could be interested in." Maybe one of them is a yoga magazine, maybe one is a travel magazine. Maybe you pick a fashion magazine or a car magazine or a *Robb Report* or *Forbes* or any topic to help you start thinking bigger.

Once I was flabbergasted to hear, "What's Barnes and Noble?" That response kind of took me aback. If you have a lack of exposure, it's imperative that you confront it. A lot of you are afraid of selling higher end homes because you've never been in one or you have a certain price range that you're nervous to go over. That's called lack of exposure, and it's a very curable deficit. That's why you have coaching, right? This is an example of the types of things that we deal with on coaching calls all the time. Well, maybe you're even using the good old-fashioned excuse, "I don't want to be out of balance." This is a very common statement that we hear. "I don't want to set too many goals, because I know to achieve them it's going to throw me out of balance in all these other areas of my life."

Well, I'm here to tell you that balance is a myth. Anyone who's successful at something is unbalanced about something else in life, at least part of the time. That's normal for motivated, focused, successful people. Olympic athletes are an example of this. Athletes of Olympic caliber practice 8, 10, sometimes as much as 12 hours a day. Do you think that they're absolutely balanced in all aspects of their life? No, but I guarantee you they've had to work on it. That's why they have tutors. That's why they have coaches. They work to compensate for their lack of balance. Claiming to be out of balance is an excuse for the less motivated, less accountable crowd, because it sounds like a good reason to avoid taking action. Sounds legit, but many of our top producers hear negative comments about their alleged balance issues from their would-be competitors.

Comments such as, "Yeah, she's successful but I bet she never sees her family," or "They're doing well but they probably have a terrible relationship," or "I bet he doesn't keep much money after running that big team." These are all accusations suggesting that one is out of balance. One of my personal coaching clients heard, "Bet you never see your boys since you're so busy," at an awards banquet. Her response was great. I was so proud of her when she responded, "Actually, I am very busy, but I'm still able to spend plenty of time with my boys. I take them on amazing vacations, and they also know that their college is paid for. They're learning that it takes hard work to succeed in life. We're doing very well together as a family, thank you," and she then proceeded to walk out of the room.

This is a common excuse justified by the non-motivated. Balance by itself is a mythical concept; no one can ever be in balance all the time with everything. However, working on balance is something real to do. It's a valid way of organizing your goals. Let's turn this into some practical applications.

How do you get serious about your goals? Well, to begin, it's useful to write down five areas on which to focus your goal setting. They are family, financial, physical, spiritual, and educational. These should be SMART goals, as we previously discussed. The way we coach goal setting has been validated and is so effective that I feel obligated to issue a warning sign here in the book: Be careful what you wish for!

Not all your goals are going to be accomplished overnight, but having them and writing them down is that critical first step to realizing them. In our dining room is a framed picture of a drawing that Tim made when he was probably 12 or 13 years old. He drew a picture of what his dream house would look like. Here we are, nine or ten houses later, we are in real estate after all, and we like to buy, sell, move up, and flip houses.

It's crazy how similar our current house is to the house he drew all those years ago. Our current home has the gardens, the river setting, and many other details, including building materials that Tim included in his picture. So, be careful what you wish for!

Let's use Lance and Karen Kenmore, a couple whom we've coached for over 10 years, as an example, because they are intensely focused at goal setting. They know when they set a goal of selling 317 houses, that nearly every time, they reach within two or three of selling that number. Remember the bow and arrow's trajectory illustration? Lance and Karen are so good at goal setting they get almost exactly what they're looking for.

Harris Highlights: Lance & Karen

"We were pushed into the habit of goal setting by great coaches early on in our lives. I think it probably started in college at a very high level. Karen and I were both college athletes and we always had very specific goals, times, objectives and routines that we followed. This program translated very well for us into the world of real estate. Once we had real estate coaches doing that same thing that our college coaches had done, it was just a continuation of that habit. One of the best things we learned early on was not to have a transaction number goal just for the sake of transactions. We were taught to create our ideal life, put a price tag on that lifestyle and then work the dollars and transactions backwards from that lifestyle.

The next level of this training for our brain was to turn these goals into a visual that was in front of us every day. If you have this board or picture up in your office or where you prospect, you can't help but think about it. It still amazes me how well this works to this day. We built a house that looks almost exactly like the plans we had on our board, we have traveled to exotic locations, bought cars, taken family vacations, and paid off debt all because of what was on our vision board. We make our kids update them once a year, and we coach our staff to do the same." – Lance & Karen Kenmore *(see Appendix for photo of their dream board)*

Goal setting should be taken very seriously. Consider what you stand to gain by seriously setting goals and ignoring those little voices in your head saying, "Well, I'm just not a goal setter. I don't want to be out of balance. What if I fall short? I don't want to feel like a failure." Squelch those negative thoughts and focus instead on what you stand to gain. Focus on what it would be like to achieve your dreams. What would it be like to set an example for your friends and your family, to think bigger and to do bigger, to be a superstar?

Focus on meeting or exceeding your goals in the five areas you listed earlier.

CHAPTER 3

Scarcity Vs. Abundance

RULE #3: There's Enough Pie for Everyone!

Tim Harris maintains if you aren't yet making the money to satisfy your dreams and ambitions, it just means you haven't yet learned that your highest and truest purpose is to be of service to others. When you live by that belief, naturally you will want to learn as much as you can to help as many people as you can.

Stephen Covey, renowned businessman and author of, *The 7 Habits of Highly Effective People*, says: "Most people are deeply scripted in what I call the Scarcity Mentality. They see life as having only so much, as though there were only one piece of pie out there. And if someone else gets the bigger piece of the pie it means less for everyone else. So, the Scarcity Mentality is the zero-sum paradigm of life. People with a Scarcity Mentality have a very difficult time sharing recognition and credit, power or profit, even with those who help them in the production of it. They also have a very hard time being genuinely happy for the success of other people."

Okay, so how do we apply this? If you have the mindset of scarcity, you believe that money, friends, success, and promotion are all scarce. You believe that there simply aren't enough of these things for everyone to have a chance at them. This affects your thoughts, your actions, your outlook, as well as the perception you have of everyone else's motives. If you're scarcity-minded, your thoughts revolve around not having enough, not being enough, and usually you also tend to think that this isn't your fault. There's a strong sense of victimhood if you have this mindset.

The scarcity mindset inhibits you from saving. You find it challenging to save both time and money because to your way of thinking, both of them are scarce. If you have either, you spend them immediately before something occurs to diminish them. Regarding real estate, it's an interesting dichotomy, because when commissions seem too scarce, you tend towards the more aggressive side, which sometimes serves you well, but often bites you in the designer business suit.

Although there are many more, in our years of coaching we've created a list of 12 factors to recognize if you're a scarcity-minded person in your real estate practice. If you answer yes to half of these, you have a mindset challenge that must be corrected before you'll be able to get to the next level. That's part of the purpose of this book — to get you through those mindset issues, help you identify what you must work on, so that you're free to move to that next level. We're clearing out the cobwebs here.

Answer yes or no to the following 12 statements to know whether you may be scarcity-minded:

1. You have no savings. Ever. If you do save, it may last only for a couple of weeks. Sometimes only for a couple of minutes.

2. You believe there's only so much money to go around and often get into conflict over commissions, both with clients and with other agents.

3. You don't use buyer's agency because you're afraid of losing the commission to an agent who doesn't use buyer's agency agreements.

4. You lose listings over things like sticking to your guns on commissions. You'd rather be right or righteous than give a little to make a deal happen. That's making it all about you, not all about your seller prospect.

5. You're immune to goal setting and feel you're above it. Goal setting just isn't for you.

6. You feel that if someone else succeeds, they've taken something off your plate.

7. You often get outbid on competitive buyer offers because you feel for the buyer's "not having enough to go high enough to win." Then you blame the buyer, the market, the other agent or the seller for your deal not happening. If you do get something in contract, it's always because of you, your expertise, experience and abilities. No one else is given credit or congratulations by you if you are scarcity-minded.

8. You're always doing free training, and 30-day free trials versus investing in actual education. You are virtually un-coachable.

9. You're a skeptic. Everyone is just out to make a buck versus trying to help you, or support you or provide a legitimate service to you. You already know everything, anyway.

10. You tend to be a grudge holder. It's also never your fault, ever, for any reason.

11. You feel the world owes you and you're being cheated. Others perceive you as negative and even angry.

12. You hate doing what you don't want to do when you don't have to do it, and you rarely do it at a high level, if you do it at all.

Wow! It's exhausting just talking about being scarcity-minded. Do these 12 points zap your energy the way they zap mine? Imagine what it's like to have a few coaching calls in a row like this. But it's our job to move you forward, so you'll never catch our coaches getting into this kind of mud with you. Failure is not an option. It's only a matter of how much success and how quickly we can get you out of your scarcity-mindedness.

Even talking about scarcity is exhausting. Let's get on to the good stuff — the positive, abundance mindset. Stephen Covey says, "The Abundance Mentality on the other hand, flows out of a deep inner sense of personal worth and security. It's the paradigm that there is plenty out there and enough to spare for everybody. It results in sharing of prestige, of recognition, of profits, of decision-making. It opens possibilities, options, alternatives and creativity."

When you have a mindset of abundance, you believe and operate knowing that there is enough for everyone. Your core belief centers on being of service to others. You know in your heart of hearts that you help enough people at a high enough level, and you relax, knowing you will always have an abundance of income.

Because you believe there is enough, your outlook is more positive both inwardly, towards yourself, as well as outwardly, toward others. Even when things don't go your way, you're looking for the silver lining instead of looking for the black cloud. Abundance-minded coaching clients are often in the flow of business, meaning they find momentum easier in the first place and easier to maintain it once they've found it. They're clear on their goals and on their ability to reach them, if they stay in the mindset of service.

There are 12 ways you know you've got the mindset of abundance in real estate. Your exercise is to compare how many mindset items you have under the scarcity list versus under the abundance list.

Answer the following 12 statements yes or no to find out whether you may be abundance-minded.

1. You have and believe in your goals. You've spent considerable time thinking about what it is you want this business to provide for you and your family. You are in relentless pursuit of these goals.

2. You have a media-free morning and a media-free life as much as possible. You know that your reality is what you create versus reacting to what you hear on the news or what someone says to you. You are the master of your trajectory.

3. You are coachable. You're non-resistive to criticism, direction and education. You don't act like you already know everything, even though you do have killer knowledge and experience in many cases.

4. You are joyful, giving, and grateful. You're a pleasure to know and to do business with.

5. You change and are flexible with your market. You don't say things like, "I hate buyers," or "I don't even show short sales," or other income-defeating limitations.

6. Failure is not an option for you. It's not even a consideration.

7. You know that when someone succeeds, it doesn't mean that you've failed. You celebrate their success and you congratulate them. You see what you can learn from them instead of feeling defeated.

8. You listen to podcasts and audiobooks and read continuously to upgrade your mindset and your education.

9. You're forgiving of others but also admit to mistakes. You take responsibility and correct your own course of action as needed.

10. You always put your clients' interests first.

11. You're confident, but not arrogant.

12. You don't believe that the world owes you; you believe that you're here to serve the world. You don't take issue with doing what you don't want to do when you don't want to do it. You do it at the highest level possible with pleasure.

Below are some simple rules that you can follow to help put you into an abundance mindset now that you understand the difference between that one and the scarcity mindset. They are easy to do.

1. Keep a gratitude journal. No matter what happens every day, write down at least three things you're grateful for. Even if you just write that it was sunny and you had a great cappuccino, you're keeping yourself in gratitude and away from grumbling. The scarcity-minded broker agents are always negative. That's no way to attract business.

2. Keep yourself in the mindset of giving versus what you're here to get. Your commission income is the direct result of your ability to help people buy and sell property in such a way that they achieve their goals. Your goals result from theirs. The better you are at providing the highest level of service, the more people you can help. The more you help them, the more you make. Concentrate more on how you make your prospects and clients feel and less on how the process makes you feel.

    This is a big point we make in coaching. Some of you feel that your success is related to how you feel every day, how the business is making you feel, how your deals are making you feel. Remember, it's not about you. American poet and author Maya Angelou once said, "I've learned that people will forget what you said, people will forget what you did, but people will never forget how you made them feel."

3. Make certain to associate with roses, and not with roaches. You can control what you put into your head. This means reducing the media noise around you, ending toxic relationships, prequalifying prospects so you don't work with people who won't ever buy or sell or who are too full of conflict for you to reasonably work with.

4. Control what goes into your mind, your body and your wallet. If you can control your thinking, your health and your income, you're on the path to abundance. Curiously, we found in coaching that once you become proficient at one of these three things, the other two fall into place much more easily. It's all about discipline and managing your mindset. Clients who become great at their physical fitness for example, and their nutrition, are almost always the same clients who are fiscally sound, mentally strong and on track with their goals.

5. Control your environment. Organizing your home, your office and your car will get you into the mindset of abundance you already have all around you. Filtering through the clutter of your physical environment does fantastic things to filter your thoughts as well. One of the first things we do in coaching is to take a "before" picture of your working environment. Sometimes that's your home office, sometimes it's your car, office, or another location. But the "after" picture always gets you into production. It's one of the easiest ways to get you making money and fixing your mindset challenges at the same time. So many of you have said, "Now that I have a working environment, I can make some money."

6. Be coachable. A great coach helps you see your strengths and pulls more out of those things that you're already great at. That same coach helps you identify weaknesses and helps you overcome them. The coach also knows which items to work on and in what order. Always be coached by someone who has actually done what you're trying to accomplish, not just someone has read about

coaching, or has coached in some other industry. Sometimes, it's not you, it's the coach.

7. Be okay with making a lot of money. Don't take this action item for granted. You may have reverse scarcity issues, that when you have a great month, a great quarter or a great year, you might have some wealth guilt. You made so much that it must have been at someone else's expense. That gets you right back into that scarcity. You better spend all that money before it goes away. That's reverse scarcity. Remember, with an abundance mindset, there's plenty to go around. If you don't become okay with wealth, with profit, with success, you won't ever have any of those things.

8. Begin to associate with others who are both wealthy and stable, as well as abundance-minded.

9. Post your goals in an obvious location, where you will see them daily. Replace, revamp and upgrade your goals as you achieve them.

10. Recommended reading:

Ego is the Enemy, Ryan Holiday
The Big Leap: Conquer Your Hidden Fear and Take Life to the Next Level, Guy Hendrix
Fanatical Prospecting, Jeb Blount

Harris Highlights: What Superstar Collette McDonald Learned about Urgency and Abundance

Before I started coaching with Tim and Julie I was like most mildly successful people. I was just successful enough to think that I could let calls go to voicemail, give clients times to meet that were days away from when we first spoke, and procrastinate about the tasks I really despised, like speaking with sellers as to why their homes were not selling. I had some false sense of reasoning that as long as I got back to a hot lead, past client or even current client within 24 hours, that was good enough. When Julie asked me to start doing the following, it was a game changer:

- **Answer Your Phone!** I know that sounds stupidly simple but I was particularly good at letting calls go to voicemail if it was not the most PERFECT time or environment in which to answer a call. I changed my mindset, that when my phone rang unless I was with my family at dinner, church, or reading stories before bed, I was going to answer that call. I involved my kids in that mindset, turning it into a game so that they would know that answering the phone meant putting food on the table and being around for their most formative years.

- **Make the Appointment for Today!** Potential clients are taken aback when you offer to meet with them that day or the next. This is an important life event for the client and they want to know you have the energy and the time for them. Most of the time the potential client cannot meet that quickly, but the energy and enthusiasm of actually trying to get in their schedule leaves a lasting impression.

- **Write the Contract NOW!** It does not matter if you are in a fast market or a slow market, you write the contract as soon as humanly possible. It sets the expectation for the client that there is urgency on all parts. It may mean you miss a family function or are late, but you must get that contract in before your client changes their mind or the house is gone. The same goes when listing a property. You do not leave that house until you have a commitment on the next steps.

- **Eat the Frog Early!** It's true, no matter what your situation is. When there is a task that you are dreading, do it first so that it doesn't weigh on you and screw up your mindset for the day. You are a professional getting paid to handle the problems, not just cashing in the check at closing.

It may seem basic but the concept of urgency is how I live my life now not just professionally, but personally as well. It's better to be urgent and efficient so that you can afford to relax and enjoy the fruits of your labors instead of stressing that you have not done enough to provide stability for yourself and your family.

CHAPTER 4

Daily Habits of a Top Producer

RULE #4: Your Profit Is Your Product

Everyone struggles with how to manage or "control" their time and not be overwhelmed. The secret is to focus on the things that matter and let the other things go.

It's important to recognize that your daily schedule should always be based on profit. Lead with profit, always. That's one of the main tenets of Tim and Julie Harris Real Estate Coaching. Specifically, the things that you must act on daily have to lead to profit.

Memorize this list. It is in chronological order. Lead generation is first, since no leads means nothing else really matters. You always have to start with lead-generation. After lead-generation comes lead follow-up, prequalify, present, negotiate and close. Then we say, "lather, rinse, repeat." These are the things that make you money or profit in your real estate practice. If it's not on that list, why are you doing it? The most common profit-killing, schedule-wrecking activities of all agents, regardless of their market, experience or their price range are the following:

1. No morning control of time. Getting to work when you finally can get to work is not a plan. That's what hobbyists do, they fit it in when they get to it. And that's why they make hobbyist money.

2. Getting stuck in the weeds of transaction coordination. Get a transaction coordinator. It's part of the cost of each transaction built in, or you should be, at least, mentally building into the cost of the transaction; it's well worth it to maintain your sanity and to buy your time back. Most transaction coordinators range between about $250 per file up to $550 maybe $600 per file depending on your price range, your market and your standards. We recommend TrusteTC.com for a virtual transaction coordinator.

3. Wasting time on social media, pretending that it's generating leads for you — another common mistake.

4. Going to appointments that you don't have to go to. Home inspections, lender lunches, free trainings… if it's not on the dollar-productive list of activities, it is not a necessary appointment. You're just hiding out pretending to work. We always remind our coaching clients if we were to put an agent cam on you and film all of the activities you do during the day when you're falling into these bad habits, and send it to your spouse or significant other, they probably wouldn't believe that you are a professional full-time real estate agent.

The above list contains the activities you're no longer allowed to do. If this is a challenge, make a deal with your spouse, your kids, and your assistant, that every time they catch you doing any of these, they get a crisp $100 bill. That'll cure you, and usually fairly quickly. If that's not enough, because you're making too much for $100 to be painful, make it $500, make it $1000, until you're clear that you're not being profitable when you engage in those schedule-wrecking activities.

Let's get back to what you must do daily instead of what you must not do to meet or exceed your goals in the five areas of life that we discussed earlier. It all starts with generating leads in the first place. You might have the most polished listing presentation in the whole world or the most amazing buyer pre-qualification script, but with no leads, it doesn't matter.

If you are lead-generation challenged, refer to our Survival Guide, our Treasure Map or our 90-Day Massive Action Plan, included in our Premier Coaching Program. Remember to focus, F-O-C-U-S is the word, that means, "Follow one course until successful." Don't do the 90-Day Massive Action Plan for nine days and then give up. Ask for help if you need it.

A person's good habits exhibited in his or her morning routine set the tone for the rest of the day. Those good habits can be further reflected in one's schedule, body, mind and wallet!

After you've browsed through your bank accounts, reviewed your investments, set your mindset on a positive trajectory and worked out, it's time to get on with the business day. Don't skip any of the key rules that we've already discussed. If you're struggling with this, perfect your pre-work routine before conquering your daily work schedule.

What follows is our recommended, ideal schedule. We define ideal as meaning that you follow it four out of five working days every week that you're not on vacation. We like to be realistic, so we expect it to be kept four out of five working days.

Schedule Rules

6:30 a.m. Get up! Powerful affirmations, 20 or 30-minute simple workout, eight ounces of water, review your goals for the day. Keep it simple.

7:00 a.m. Make a 30-minute quick financial review. Are you trending up or down versus your financial goals? Are you on track? Are you ahead? Are you behind? By how much, ahead or behind? Look at your whiteboards, as we teach you in the Premier class, and your Vital Signs

Report. What is your appointment schedule? What appointments must you set today? What appointments are you going on today? Note to self at this point, you're honoring our previous chapter, where we talked about controlling your mind, your body and your wallet, and it's not even 7:00 a.m. yet!

7:00-8:00 a.m. Prepare for your day. Breakfast, shower, dress. When in doubt, dress for success! Be dressed one level nicer than your prospect or your client. If you're not sure, based on your appointments, maybe you've never met them before, err on the side of one step nicer.

8:00 a.m. Take 20 minutes to clear out any mission-critical email, voicemail, texts, and respond to anything else that's imperative — in 20 minutes, that's it. Set a timer. Delete all trash and spam. Delegate anything you can to your transaction coordinator or personal assistant. If you don't have a transaction coordinator, or a personal assistant, you are your transaction coordinator or personal assistant, which means you have even more critical time here to spend that same 20 minutes, prioritized by urgency, and set a plan in place. Maybe that means you're going to devote an hour this afternoon when you don't have appointments to conquering whatever you uncovered that you have to do. But don't do it at this point. That's where most of you make a mistake. You get sucked into the drama, and then the rest of your schedule is a train wreck. Use this 20 minutes to just figure out what's mission-critical.

8:30-9:00 a.m. Relentless lead follow-up, with intent to set appointments. This is the most critical point in your day. Not just following up on leads, not just, "Hey, how's it going?" It's relentless lead follow-up with intent to actually set appointments. That is the point of lead follow-up. Since you're most likely to set an appointment with this category of prospects, it's valuable to pursue them first thing in your day. You have their phone numbers, they're expecting your call, and you have what they want — information about listing their home, or property to show them if they're buyers. Remember to prequalify all listing and buyer leads prior to setting that appointment. Don't skip this step or you'll find yourself wasting more time on appointments you shouldn't be on. You should never, ever end the day, or even end the morning with leads that you've not followed-up on, using our proven lead follow-up scripts. We have scripts for following up on expireds, open house leads; you name it, we have lead follow-up scripts.

9:30 a.m. More lead follow-up, if you have the leads to follow up on. If not, it's time for lead-generation. Consider the following: let's say you have an endless supply of leads, as some of you do from your different spokes that you've set up over the years, maybe you've got a huge past client or center-of-influence list, and they're feeding you referrals, you've got tons of leads, for whatever reason. It doesn't make sense to put pressure on yourself to create a new marketing piece or to learn how to hardcore prospect. After that, choose your most likely to list spokes first. This means unrepresented sellers, otherwise known as for sale by owners, expireds, probate, etc. It makes sense to speak with people who need what it is you do. Remember, if you've generated enough leads to follow up on, do that first. For more on this, refer to our 18 Lead Follow-Up Rules (see Appendix).

10:30 a.m. Call your required past client center-of-influence list. That's usually for most agents between three and five contacts. You might have to dial ten times to get those five contacts, but here's how you do it. You take the total number of people on your list, you divide that number by either 20 working days, 40 working days or 60, and that'll help you determine how many people you'll have as your minimum call standard every day, so that you can contact that list every 90 days or less. The example is, if you have 100 people with real phone numbers on your past client and sphere list and divide that by 20 working days, (in every 30-day month), then you'll have to speak with just five people a day to touch your entire list every month. What would your business be like then? I can tell you, generally 20-30 percent better than it is now, assuming that you do this religiously as part of your schedule.

11:30 a.m. Assess your day so far. Have you set any appointments yet? If you have set no appointments, proceed to continued lead follow-up and/or prospecting.

12:30 Lunch. Real lunch. Don't skip lunch. It's not a badge of honor. Actually, have lunch — ideally with a past client, a current client, or a referral client or maybe somebody else in your center of influence. Ideally you eat lunch somewhere in your market where you can be out and about talking about real estate, not being a secret agent.

1:30 p.m. Check in with your transactions, your team, your staff, your co-op agents. This is your hour of power to keep your existing business buttoned up, but only one hour. Some of you are using the entire day instead of only one hour. Pareto's Law says: "The task will grow to the time you give it." Give yourself an hour, that's all.

2:00-5:00 p.m. Appointment time. If you don't have any appointments, you have options, but they all center around creating income. Appointments are best, after that it's time for calling your sellers, setting up showings, previewing, doing price reductions, scheduling open houses, creating market plans. Ideally, it's back to your lead follow-up and preparing for tomorrow's appointments, but if you get bored or unproductive with your normal routine, since this is somewhat flexible, break out of it by going after a new spoke like probate or new construction, for rent by owners, or any other new category. Maybe a new area for your center of influence and signing up for other meetings so that you can meet more people.

5:00-6:00 p.m. Time to tie down loose ends. If you don't have a quitting time, it won't be 5:00, it'll be midnight when you do this. Stick to your schedule. Any negotiations should be resolved and sent to the other side so that they will owe you a response in the morning, not the other way around. Don't have contracts open until 9:00 a.m. the following morning or dealing with home inspections that you have to know by 7:00, or whatever. It's their problem. They must get back to you and I

Would you like a FREE copy of Tim and Julie's proven business plan?
http://FreeCoachingCallsForAgents.com

would recommend that you set noon or 2:00 p.m. as their do-or-die time so that you're not having to deal with it first thing in the morning when you're trying to control your time.

6:00 p.m. Quitting time. (Maybe even earlier.) Get back with your family. Back to husband or wife. Back to significant other. Back to dealing with raising kids. And if none of that's going on for you, go enjoy your evening. Any of that is fine, but have a real quitting time.

Harris Rules for Business Days

1. Have a definite starting and quitting time. It should be the same time every day.

2. Never end the day with leads that you have not followed up. Frequently, the question arises, "What if I have a quitting time of 6:00 and something comes in after 6:00?" Well use your best judgement on that. If you're starving for your next deal, it's probably a good idea to follow up with them anyway and break your rule, temporarily. But you're going to make it a lot easier if your voicemail says, and you've all heard this, "If you're leaving a message after normal business hours, let me know where I can contact you the following morning." Easy enough, you're setting expectations.

3. Take care of your mind, your body and your wallet check-ins before you begin your business day. Don't take all day to do it. Take an hour or so as we discussed.

4. Have a personal standard of setting at least one pre-qualified quality appointment every day before noon.

5. Have a personal standard of going on a qualified appointment daily, so that Number Four was about setting one, Number Five is about going on one. If you get into that routine it becomes easier.

6. Speak with active listings clients once per week, at the same time, on the same day. We recommend either Friday or Monday, since going into the weekends they're wondering what you're doing with their listing and/or coming out of the weekends they're wondering the same. Use our Seller's 12-Week Communication Plan to help you with those conversations.

7. Speak with a minimum reasonable number of people from your center of influence, your past client list daily, using our Ford Script.

8. End your day with all negotiations on the other side's plate.

9. Hire a transaction coordinator once you're consistently managing more than three pending transactions simultaneously, for more than three consecutive months.

10. Ask for help from our coaches to hold you accountable to these standards and to continue to polish your money-making schedule. For more information on coaching, visit us at www.timandjulieharris.com

CHAPTER 5

Lead Generating with The Spokes

RULE #5: Don't Be a One-Spoke Wonder

It's time to demystify, simplify and distill lead-generation. Let's start with why lead-generation seems so challenging. If you speak with 10 different brokers, top-producing agents, real estate trainers, office managers, and gurus, you'll get 10 different answers regarding the best lead-generation plan. What's an agent to do? Who should you follow? Who should you listen to? This section will help clarify what you need to do and in what order you need to do it.

First, some facts about lead-generation. Every real estate practice is either marketing based and prospecting enhanced, or prospecting based and marketing enhanced. Prospecting based businesses are stronger because they aren't dependent on having a marketing budget. They're more time and skill dependent, making the agent more competitive, more confident, and more financially sound once their skills are sharpened. Marketing based, prospecting enhanced practices, conversely, are generally weaker are more stressful because the lead flow is dependent on both expenditure and effectiveness of the marketing.

Whether you decide to be prospecting or marketing based is determined by your budget, your skill level and your production needs. We'll help you figure out which is best for you. Next to consider, is whether to buy or not to buy leads. What are the pros and cons? For every licensed agent, it seems like there are hundreds of companies trying to get that agent to buy what they're selling — leads. There's an offer right now in your email, guaranteed! Some of these companies might be a good idea for you, but by no means is it a guarantee of the number, quality, or consistency of the leads that you'll get. Have you ever wondered why they're called impressions versus qualified leads? We'll address this in greater detail after the groundwork is laid for you to make good decisions. Generally, it's best to spend less on buying leads and more on sharpening your skills. Your skills are portable and predictable once you've polished them, and they're also inexpensive.

Another consideration is whether to prospect. There are pros and cons to this. Though prospecting agents have the secret power to generate, convert, and create business virtually at will, the downside is that a prospecting only business is totally dependent on that agent. It's dependent on the agent's skill, time, mindset, and schedule. Therefore, it's best to have some marketing enhancement even when you are prospecting based.

Another aspect regarding your lead-generation plan is to consider people you know versus people you don't know. In real estate, your business is dependent on two categories of people: those you know, for instance your past clients, your center of influence, relatives, etc. and those you don't, who is everyone else. Your plan will include both sides of the business. Recognize that statistically, people you already know require more contact, more frequently, than those you don't. If you are deciding to be by referral only, you'll have to make many more contacts more systematically than the agent who works both sides of the business. You'll also have to make more contacts than the agent who works only with people they don't know.

Here's an example. If you speak with 10 of your friends today, it's possible that zero of them are going to buy or sell with you in the next 90 days. If you speak with 10 expireds, for sale by owners, or probate leads, it's possible that all 10 will indeed want to sell and possibly also buy in the next 90 days. If you have one hour to spend, who should you call? The friends will be easier calls. After all, they're people whom you already know and from whom you might get a referral, but wouldn't you rather spend your time speaking with 10 people who statistically actually need your expertise? Is there one magic bullet for generating high-quality, inexpensive, pre-qualified, motivated leads? Nope. Stop looking for one.

The key to lead-generation happiness is simply to get clear on the spokes-on-the-wheel analogy and to embrace the magic of it.

Let's imagine that you've just assembled a bicycle. It looks great. It's shiny. It's red. It looks like a great bike, but it's got just one spoke in the front wheel. The spoke is strong so it seems like it should be fine. You climb on and you start pedaling away. You're cruising along at a steady pace until *wham-o*. You wipe out. What happened? You hit a little rock in the bike path. Fortunately, you recover with only a few scrapes and bruises, so you get back on and take off down the path but *wham-o*. Again, you wipe out.

This time the cause is from hitting a pothole that you didn't see until it was too late. Having one spoke on your bike is exactly like having just one strong source of business in your real estate practice. For most agents, these are referrals and/or sphere of influence clients, but the problem is that this is not an endless supply of transactions. Eventually, you'll run out of referrals, your friends will have their ultimate house until they retire or they'll just move away. Now that you're aware that one spoke isn't enough to sail along, not only for a beginner's bike path but also on a sometimes-treacherous mountain bike tour, it's time to build up your spokes.

In real estate, you must have five to eight very strong, systematized, predictable spokes, i.e. sources of business, to have a predictable, stable income. That's a fact. What if you don't see any referrals for the next 90 days or so? Not a peep from your previously strong spoke of past clients, friends, and referrals. What then? Wait around and starve? What if you have five other sources, all of which produced reliable lead flow? You'd not just be fine but you would produce even more than you "needed." Diversification creates predictable profit. This is how you meet or exceed your goals which you established earlier in this book. After you ask yourself some key questions, we'll look at the combination of spokes that we recommend and you'll have absolute clarity on what you need to begin to build.

Lose the thought that there's just one thing that you can do to solve your lead-generation challenges. The good news is that when you get your spokes built, the rest of the business is easier to systematize, easier to manage, and a pleasure to run. If you don't figure out your lead-generation wheel, everything else is harder, disorganized, and a general mess. This is one of the most important things for you to take away from this book and it's even more critical that you take action on. Here are two great stories. The first is from Tim and perfectly illustrates what can happen to an agent who relies entirely on a prospecting-based business, and also lacks the diversification that the spokes provide. The second is from one of our coaching clients who saw his business explode over a 3-year period with the spokes method.

Harris Highlights –
The One-Spoke Wonder Crisis

"A few years ago, I received a phone call from an agent who was well known in the United States as being one of the most prolific "hunters" of for sale by owners and expireds. This gal would sell 300 to 400 listings per year and she was a monster at converting those folks! But the reason she was calling me wasn't to learn more about how to prospect FSBOs and expireds. Her purpose was to share with me that if she had listened to Julie and I a few years ago on one our webinars when we talked about the Spokes-on-the-Wheel approach, it would have saved her a lot of anguish. She said had she heeded and applied our advice, it would have helped her weather one of the worst health crises of her life.

"She went on to tell me that she had developed a case of laryngitis. She went to the doctor and the doctor told her not to talk! Well, here was a gal whose only source of business was picking up the phone and converting those leads to appointments and then to listings. Well, like any ambitious prospecting agent, she didn't listen to her doctor, and continued to make calls until she couldn't talk at all! The laryngitis had gotten so bad that she was completely mute for 2 to 3 weeks. The doctor told her that if she didn't give her voice a break, she could potentially cause permanent damage to her vocal cords! That's how dedicated she was to making her prospecting calls, but that's also what happens when you only have one source of business. She was living in fear that she was only a one-spoke wonder and if she wasn't making those calls, her business was going to dry up! A justified fear too, if you ask me! So, she called to thank me for introducing her to the spokes approach and asked if I would coach her on doing just that. Of course, I said yes and she became one of my long-time great coaching clients."

Harris Highlights – The System that Tripled One Agent's Sales

"In my first year in real estate, I closed 10 deals, all of which were buyers. I also made $36,000 doing broker price opinions (or BPOs), which was my first spoke. I learned the importance of having at least four spokes going at all times in the years that followed and also, how they created diversity and stability in my income. My other spokes were open houses, expireds and later my COI, which in hindsight, should have been my first spoke.

In my second year, I added a new spoke called "investors" while maintaining all my original spokes. I ended the year doing 18 deals and having $95,000 in income. In my third year, I closed 36 deals and made $150,000. Each spoke represented a source of business, a system I used, and an opportunity to strengthen my knowledge of the market.

Currently, I run 9 spokes and have more available depending on the economic cycle we are in. Every year, my oldest daughter, Savannah, and I rewrite my spokes. It has become a ritual that reminds me why the spokes are important and why they need to be worked."

- B. Bryd

Now that you have some facts (and actual real life stories!) about your lead options and how important the spokes-on-the-wheel lead-generation method is, it's time to get introspective.

There are 10 questions to ask yourself to be able to make the right decision with your personal lead-generation plan or your personal spokes-on-the-wheel.

Would you like a FREE copy of Tim and Julie's proven business plan?
http://FreeCoachingCallsForAgents.com

1. Do I actually have a marketing budget? If so, how much is it? For many agents, you can stop right there. You're going to have to be prospecting based. If you do have such a budget, is that the amount for this week, this month, this quarter, or this year? Keep in mind that marketing works much better, when it works at all, with consistency versus sporadic spending.

2. Do I have other sources of income in addition to what I must earn in real estate? If so, how much is that income and how long am I going to get it? Consider a spouse's income, rental income, another job, a pension, or any other source.

3. Based on your work in previous chapters, what is your real income goal for your real estate practice? What do you have to make monthly to pay your bills and replace your old job, for example? Versus what do you want to make monthly to fund your new, upgraded, goal-based lifestyle?

4. Take your answer from number three above and divide by the average net commission in your marketplace. If you're not sure, use the average for the ZIP code in which you plan to sell. If you're experienced, you have your own track record so use your own average net commission. Divide into your required income figure monthly and you'll know how many transactions you need to meet or exceed your goals.

5. Do you love speaking with people or are you a bit intimidated by the idea of prospecting? Do you gravitate towards people whom you know, or whom you don't know when you think about prospecting? Either answer is fine, but it will help you determine what to pursue with your lead-generation wheel.

6. What support does your office offer you already? Some offices do have lead-generation set up and disseminate leads to the agents. Some offices have a good flow of corporate relocation, builder

relationships, or other sources. Know what's in front of you before you build your own wheel of spokes.

7. If you're an experienced agent, what has worked for you in the past and why did you stop doing it?

8. What do your current market conditions call for? What is your market looking for? Keep your marketing and prospecting appropriate to what's happening around you.

9. How many people are in your center of influence and past client database? What are you doing currently to handle their real estate needs?

10. How quickly do you need to make money in real estate? What kind of time do you have to learn, implement, and polish?

The above questions and your answers will help you decide what to pursue and when. Let your answers filter your decision-making process, so that you won't have to backtrack in your business. Then, follow our recommended spokes. For all agents, the core foundational spoke must be your database. This is your list of your past clients, your friends, your neighbors, people in your center of influence, professional contacts, and personal contacts. Ideally, your list eventually reaches 500 people for whom you have names, addresses, phone numbers, and email addresses.

Systematize your database for past client/sphere-of-influence lead-generation as we instruct below. Note this is a people-you-know spoke. Thus, it takes careful and consistent nurturing. Do not dabble with this spoke. Take your time to get it done right.

How-To:
Systematize Your Past Client Sphere of Influence "Spoke"

1. Create the list if you don't already have it using only one database like Top Producer, for example and purify your data. That step alone will take you some time if it's not already done.

2. Use automated communication to send regular emails of videos to your database. "Send it and forget it!"

3. Choose a reasonable number of people to actually speak with by phone or in person daily from your database. Five or less is recommended, though you'll need to dial a larger number to make those five real contacts. We'll do a little math example here.

4. Example: Assume 200 contacts in databases. At 10 contacts per day, you can contact 100% in 20 business days. At 5 contacts per day, you can contact 100% every 60 days.

5. One center-of-influence event per quarter. Better is one per month.

6. A seasonal gift, a stop-by during holidays for your top 20 to 50 contacts from this list.

7. Firepoint.com for enhancing your communication and staying up on relationships. The more you communicate, the more business will come from this spoke.

8. Regular center-of-influence meetings to expand your database, your relationships, your referrals. Three to five meetings per week with clubs and organizations that are interesting enough that you'll build friendships and expand your reach. For business-focused groups, we recommend Business Networking International (BNI.com), Letip. com, Young Entrepreneurs Organization (YEO.org), Entrepreneurs Organization (EONetworking.org) and Meetup.com. Here's a secret. When someone takes a listing and you ask yourself how in

the world they got it, nine times out of ten, it's because the person already knew that agent. Be the agent that they *already know*.

Fact. People choose from who they already know first, then they ask for a referral, and only after that do they respond to marketing.

When you do the above things systematically on our list, you can expect a 10-30% return on that list. Your contacts will buy or sell with you or refer someone they know to you.

Would you like a FREE copy of Tim and Julie's proven business plan?
http://FreeCoachingCallsForAgents.com

CHAPTER 6

The Magic Number Formula

RULE #6: Know Your Magic Number

What do our clients mean when they talk about a "magic number?" It is how many active listings you need to have at all times to sell the number of units to meet or exceed your income goal. This is quite possibly the most important number of your entire real estate career. In other words, how many listings do you need to create a predictable number of closings per month that matches your goal? What's magic about the number? Each listing you have should create a minimum of one additional listing and up to five additional buyers. This happens because of all of your marketing, prospecting, promotional efforts, and all that surrounds each of your active listings.

We teach you how to do this in coaching, so don't worry if you don't know how to do all of it yet. You can get the help you need, but first you have to understand what your individual magic number actually is. (Here's the secret: Listings have 10x more value to you than buyers do because of the momentum that they create. When you work with the buyer, it's one sale once and even that could be argued. Hopefully, you'll get referrals, but when you've sold a buyer his home, that's that. Listings create other business. That's why you must become a great listing agent. It also allows you to stop doing crazy things like paying for buyer leads. How do you ascertain your magic number? First, make sure that you've calculated your ultimate monthly income. Refer to your work in previous chapters here.

Do not proceed with this section unless you know how many deals per month you need to close. That's what the <u>ultimate monthly income worksheet</u> creates for you, so go back and do it if you skipped it, and ask for help if needed. The number of transactions you need monthly is what you calculated on that sheet. Memorize that number. Make sure that you've accounted for your broker's split and any other cost of each listing such as a set transaction coordination fee. Calculate it based on your net.

How do you figure out how many listings you need to create those monthly deals? You must know a little bit about the absorption rate in your marketplace. Don't freak out. It's easier than it sounds. The absorption rate is the rate at which homes are selling in a specific area. How many days or months does it take to sell an active listing? Don't get stuck on the term. It just refers to how fast or slow you can expect to sell a home given current market conditions.

Three pieces of information are necessary to find the absorption rate. They are: the specific timeframe, the number of sold homes during that timeframe, and the number of active homes now. When we talk about timeframe, that could be 90 days if your market is moving very quickly. It could be six months or maybe you take a year's worth of data, but you've got to use the same specific timeframe. That's why you start with it. Why do you care about the absorption rate? Let's say you're going to your next listing appointment and you are now able to talk to your client about the number of months' inventory of homes like this that are currently on the market. You can set expectations for how long it should take to sell based on market conditions, inventory, supply and demand.

Will this add to your pricing confidence? Will the seller be more likely to allow you to accurately price his home? Certainly. Will you be smarter and more professional than your competition? Absolutely. You're working with your next buyer. You are trusted to negotiate for the perfect house. You can then communicate to the seller's agent and to your buyer that there's a year's worth of inventory currently available on par with their listing. Conversely, you might have to advise your buyer, based on a complete lack of inventory and very low days in the market, that if they want their dream home, it's appropriate and expected that they write an offer above the list price. Either way, knowing the absorption rate gives you the confidence necessary to give sound advice to your clients.

The absorption rate is a measure of how many months' worth of homes are currently on the market. This is calculated by establishing how many purchases were made in the past 12 months within a given set of parameters. Next, we find how many homes are currently on the market with the same set of parameters by dividing the number of current listings, by the number of buyers buying per month, in other words, closings, and we arrive at the absorption rate. If, for example, there are 10 homes on the market just like your subject property and two sell per month, you have a five-month supply. In other words, you could expect it to take five months on average to sell that subject property. Now, if you've got 10 homes on the market and five sell per month, there's only a two-month supply, and if 10 of them sell per month, you have virtually no supply. In other words, you can expect that home to sell probably by midnight.

Use your MLS to pull out this data. Keep in mind that you must use the same criteria for your sold search as you do for your active search. Be specific but not too specific. Those of you who have done thousands of broker price opinions know what I mean. Here's another example. Let's say that your subject property is in the Worthington suburb of Columbus, Ohio. Don't take the numbers for all of Columbus; limit your search to just Worthington Schools. It's a standard two-story with four bedrooms and two and a half baths, and a two-car garage, and it's 2,300 square feet. It was built in the '60s. It's in an established neighborhood. I'll limit my search then to that ZIP code in Worthington Schools with four bedrooms, two and a half baths, and give it a little range of between 2,000 square feet to 2,600 square feet, and search for solds in the past 12 months.

In other words, I'm being specific, but not super specific. Next, I divide the total number of solds that are similar to my subject property by 12 and that tells me how many homes like that sell per month. If there are a 120 sold in 12 months, the market absorbs, meaning, someone buys, 10 of those homes per month. We then use the same criteria to see how many homes like my subject property are currently for sale or active listings and I divide actives by solds. If I have 20 active listings and 10 sell per month, that would be two months' supply or I can expect to have about 60 days in the market. If I have 10 homes for sale like my subject property and 10 sell per month, it's likely going to sell pretty fast.

All of this does not take into account any new homes coming on to the market, so it's important to run these numbers regularly to see what's really happening. A couple of secrets illustrate this. Secret number one, two suburbs in the same town can have dramatically different absorption rates and even within that subdivision itself, if there are more or less desirable factors. Factors such as schools, parks, development, and desirability, all have an effect on the number of days or months it takes to sell housing inventory. Secret number two, the National Association of Realtors defines a balance market as five months' worth of inventory. Higher than five months indicates a buyer's market and lower than five months indicates a seller's market. How does this affect my personal magic number or the number of listings that I must have in inventory at all times to meet or exceed my goals? The absorption rate of your own listing inventory should reflect the same numbers as the market in which you're selling.

Generally speaking, if you're selling very high-end luxury homes, usually it's going to take longer. If you're selling nothing but first-time buyer homes, your averages might be a little bit different that way, too. In general, it means that if your area has a 60-day absorption rate for the types of homes that you sell or hope to sell as you become a better listing agent, your average days on the market should be the same or better. If it's longer, you need to work on two things: prequalifying your sellers for motivation and being great at pricing. These are both areas that you can improve in through the coaching program. Here's the big question. What is happening in your market? Does it take 10 active listings to sell two per month and get two buyers to spin off from that inventory?

The general rules have always been this: One to five listings equal about one closing per month, maybe occasionally two or three, sometimes zero. Again, it depends on your market conditions. This is how you get stuck going from deal to deal, never having predictable income. It's the most stressful time in your career to have only five or fewer listings. Once you have five active listings at all times, you can usually count on one to two closings per month. In some markets, all five will close, but that's unusual. Ten active listings at all times will guarantee you two to four closings per month, sometimes more. I'm being a bit conservative here. Fifteen active listings at all times will get you four to six closings per month and so on. Here's the secret. We're talking about active listings here, not pendings, not the short sales you had in inventory forever that are allegedly closing.

There's another secret. Some of you are in very low-inventory markets and that puts pressure on you to have more listing leads if your listings sell immediately. Your job is to replace the listings immediately upon selling, if not before. In the case of very hot markets, you'll start tracking your pipeline, your pre-listing inventory, almost as if it's actual listing inventory. Here's some homework to complete on this topic. Do an absorption rate study on a subject property you know best — your own home. As an exercise, figure out what would happen if you put it on the market today. How long would it take to sell? Next, do absorption rate studies on all of your active listings. If any of them have been on the market for longer than the average days on the market for their neighborhood, you are overpriced.

To determine if you are on the right track, figure out how many listings you must have in inventory to create predictable closings every month, which meets your ultimate income per month.

Let's look at a hypothetical agent, Jack. Jack is the guy who goes from deal to deal. He has built a pretty good business, and is able to pay his bills most months, no problem, but it seems like three or four times every year, he is temporarily broke or at least, is suffering from poor cash flow. Jack has a basic monthly income requirement of $5,000 to pay for his mortgage, car lease, cash and groceries for his family. He makes his money by either a buyer closing almost every month or selling a listing almost right away when he has a listing. If any problems occur with his one or two pending deals, he suffers the consequences by having to go into serious survival mode for up to a month while he sells something else or saves his deals.

Jack gets his bills caught up right before the next round of monthly bills comes in. This causes Jack stress. Jack has just figured out that if he had five listings at all times, he could change his career from one of subsistence to being able to save some money, take an occasional vacation with his family and sleep better at night knowing that he wasn't dependent on one or two deals. Jack needs 15,000 per month to reach his ultimate monthly income goal and pay his debts, catch up his taxes, create some financial reserves, have some fun in life and keep current on all his bills. That requires not one closing per month, but three every month. Jack pays his bills most of the time going from deal to deal. The next level for him is to make it his mission in life to build his current listing inventory to five active.

Once Jack gets to five listings, it's smooth sailing. He then simply has to replace his listings as they sell. The fact that he has five listings alone will make this dramatically easier, provided he puts a few marketing and prospecting items in place for each of those listings. He's learning how to do this in the coaching program.

Jenny is another hypothetical agent who can turn lemons into lemonade. She's a grizzled veteran. She was smart enough to have some money saved during the real estate crash and got into REOs and short sales just before she spent all of those savings. Jenny has always had two or three short sales going and, ultimately, gets them closed eventually, but she's still working on getting it done faster. It's hard for her to predict the closing dates on those types of listings.

Meanwhile, Jenny was doing a lot of REO work in her town for two or three years, and had her own little real estate boom happening. The average sale prices weren't what she was used to in the boom, but the volume made up for it. She was super busy for a while but didn't really build new relationships with asset managers or portfolio managers and her market heated up in the meantime. Her REO inventory is dwindling. Jenny hasn't really worked on normal business while she was busy with short sales and REOs, and has been so busy scrambling to take care of the volume of deals necessary at the lower price point that she's almost forgotten how to handle equity sellers. Unfortunately, she hasn't spoken to her former clients in years. Jenny isn't broke, but she's not ready to retire yet either and she's wondering what's next for her in the emerging new market.

Jenny fantasizes about what it would be like to have listing inventory again with the equity sellers in a decent price range. She set a goal of building up new inventory to at least 10 new listings in the next 90 days. She knows how to do it; she just needs to get back in the saddle. Now that Jenny sees the math and remembers how it worked in the old days, she's re-inspired to do what it takes to, once again, be the best listing agent in her area. She's going to make sure her whiteboards are set up and to get to work immediately on building listing inventory.

Chris is our third hypothetical agent, and is brand-spanking new in real estate. He really couldn't be any greener, but he's a pretty smart guy. He gets that it's a number's game, and he sees that the more people he helps to sell their homes, the more consistent income he has. He doesn't have any baggage from previous markets; he just wants to get to work.

Chris decides to call all of his friends, family, and previous associates to see who they know who wants to buy or sell a home. He knows he has a lot to learn but he's ready to get started as soon as possible. Chris figures he should learn some scripts and how to prequalify, present, and negotiate with real people so he can earn while he learns.

The final hypothetical agent is Elizabeth, who has a thriving business, a team with three buyer agents, one transaction coordinator and a personal assistant. She is well-respected as a top producer in her area. Why does she care about a magic number? She wants to take it to the next level. Elizabeth knows her own absorption rate. She knows that when she has 20 listings at all times, she and her team are able to close four transactions each and every month, and sometimes they have months with as many as six or eight closings.

Her concern is that she'd really like to plan ahead for retirement. The boom and bust cycle cleaned out her reserves, she sold her rentals, and downsized everything. Elizabeth is in rebuilding mode. She wants to rebuild her net worth, her retirement funds and buy a beach house on the coast just as she had almost been able to do during the boom prior to the last crash. She knows that the magic number is the key to happiness. Elizabeth has set a goal of doubling her listing inventory within six months and maintaining an inventory at a higher level without hiring more staff. They all could be busier and better at converting leads into appointments.

Example number five is you. What's your story? Are you struggling? Are you subsisting? Are you thriving but not consistently? Are you in rebuilding mode? Find your magic number and use your whiteboards.

Your active listings board has to have the number of listings written on the left-hand side of the board. If you average five but now have determined that you have to have 10 to reach your ultimate monthly income, then write one to 10 and fill in your existing five. Set a goal of when you'll have 10. Remember our goal-setting section. Next, it's all about how you're going to do it. That's why you're in a coaching program and that's why you're reading this book, but the secret is at least now you know exactly what the goal is. This is golden information critical to your future's success. If you have any confusion on this whatsoever, ask for help immediately.

CHAPTER 7

Become a Listing Agent, Part I

RULE #7: Listings Are Mental Labor, Buyers Are Physical Labor... List to Last!

As discussed in the previous chapter, while your real estate practice must be based on your magic number for your business to thrive, there is another major aspect on which to focus. Listings. You have to list to last. Listings are mental labor; working with buyers is physical labor. Without becoming a powerful listing agent, your business will simply reach its limit. That limit is determined by your time, your energy, and even the availability of inventory to sell to those buyers. Freedom comes with listings. You can simply handle more listing business than buyer business, once you understand the process.

How many buyers can you work with at any given time? Let's say you have five pre-approved, highly motivated buyers who all want to see property this week. You can do it, but you'll have little time for anything else and at the end of the week, you could have anywhere from no new sales to five new pending sales to manage if you're lucky. You'll then have to deal with either an intense week of showings if they didn't buy, or a month full of home inspections, termite reports, and financing issues if they did buy.

What happens next? It's the rollercoaster ride known as your personal finances. You'll either stay on the buyer hamster wheel or you'll spend all your time taking care of your pending deals, ensuring that you have a great month this month followed by a broke month next month. It's no way to live, but many agents have been told, incorrectly, that it's just a way of life when you're a salesperson on commission. Becoming a great listing agent is what catapults you out of that sad reality into the life of your dreams.

Let's now pretend that you have five highly motivated sellers and because they're motivated, they have allowed you to price their homes such that they will sell. Already, you're doing better because you have more time to spend on your lead follow-up, your lead-generation, not to mention time with your family. Once the listing is secured, the rest of your board of realtors goes to work for you showing and selling those listings. They now are doing the physical labor for you.

However, to accomplish this, you must systematize each part of your listing process. Listing agents make a lot more money, more consistently and with less stress. They have more time and more freedom than agents who never learned this critical skill. Listings are scalable, meaning you can have more without adding more time requirements. It's a more efficient, effective, and predictable way to run your business.

In this chapter, we will first discuss the basics and then cover more advanced listing agent secrets. Develop the mindset of a listing agent. Listing agents know how to consistently generate listing leads. They follow up on those leads, prequalify them, then present to them in such a way that they will take the listing, negotiate it to a sale, and close the deal. They follow a system. They're able to do all of that in such a way that the seller increases referrals to them and trusts that agent with future business.

Every listing agent should be mindful of the Seven P's. The first P refers to profit. Profit comes from previewing, prequalifying, preparing, the pre-listing presentation, and a polished, professional presentation. Norman Vincent, that progenitor of positive thinking reminds us to "Believe in yourself! Have faith in your abilities! Without a humble but reasonable confidence in your own powers, you cannot be successful or happy." But to be a successful listing agent requires something beyond belief; it requires implementation of some practical tips. And prayer doesn't hurt!

Polish your moments of truth. A moment of truth is a snap judgment, positive or negative, that a prospect or client makes about you or your business based on a sliver of information. You can control most of those snap judgments, which can greatly impact the outcome of your appointments. Some simple moments of truth are non-negotiable. If any of these things are less than optimum, you could lose the listing or the relationship.

The following is a deceptively simple checklist for an agent to follow. That being said, it's astonishing how many do not adhere to it.

Harris Listing Process Rules

1. Always prequalify.

2. Never go to an appointment when you don't know the price the seller has in mind, the motivation for the move, and move's ideal timeframe.

3. Always send your pre-listing package. No exceptions! Not having one is unacceptable.

4. Be on time for the appointment. On time is late, early is on time, and late means you lose. (This cannot be overstated.)

5. Have the best pre-listing package and the best listing presentation of anyone in your market. (Tip: Get help with this if you're struggling.

Our coaches specialize in helping you be the best in any market, in any price range.)

6. Have a firm, confident handshake. A handshake at the door is expected; it's the universal business greeting. It's a moment of truth. Are you a bone crusher or a wet fish hand shaker? Both are wrong. Here's a tip: A good handshake goes like this: Keep your fingers together with your thumb up and open, slide your hand into the other person's so each person's web of skin touches and squeeze firmly. Your handshakes should be firm but not bone crushing, last about three seconds, include good eye contact with the other person and should be released after the shake, even if the introduction conversation continues. It should feel close but assertive.

   When someone shakes with their hand facing down, it means that they want to control you. If they shake with their hand facing up, it means they're submissive. If you want to go the extra mile and convey confidence, try anchoring the handshake. This means using your other hand to touch the person softly on their forearm between their wrist and their elbow. When you do it correctly, this move gives an impression that you're fully committed to speaking with the person. Just be sure not to go any higher than the elbow, as this could make the person feel like you're invading their personal space.

   When do you shake hands? Meeting somebody for the first time, meeting someone you haven't seen for a while, greeting your host or hostess, greeting guests, saying goodbye to people at a gathering, or when someone else extends their hand.

7. Stand up straight when you're meeting people. Sit confidently at the presentation table. On this we agree with your mother or grandmother, whoever originally made this point to you. Hunching or slouching isn't just bad for your posture; it's really bad for business.

The subconscious message you send when you're in a less than perfect posture is a lack of confidence, trustworthiness, and sincerity. Uneven body language sends the message of indecisiveness. Do you see a curve or a straight line in your back? Stand up straight. Correct uneven shoulders or an uneven front end profile — that's not really an image that you want to portray. It's a moment of truth.

Tip: Keep a mirror in your office. Are you standing up straight? Look at your side profile in the mirror. If you're leaving your car for an appointment, look at your reflection in the windows.

8. Be fidget free; don't annoy your prospects. Fidgeting is displayed in many ways, but they all say the same thing: You're uncomfortable. Watch for it in yourself, as you watch for it in your prospects. You know it when you see it. This can be during the presentation; playing with your hair, tapping your foot incessantly, scratching, folding your arms, messing with your tie, checking your cellphone, touching your jewelry. It's all fidgeting, and it sends the wrong message.

How do you fix it? You should have a strategy that you deploy when you feel uncomfortable. Take a breath, say an affirmation to yourself, set your hands on the table or in your lap and feel your feet planted firmly on the ground. Think of a role model for your presentation style. Audrey Hepburn is my favorite, but coaching clients have mentioned various actors, actresses, sportscasters, etc. Notice that they don't fidget; they have an air of confidence. They don't present as insecure or uncomfortable. Have some mini-scripts to slow yourself down during the presentation, such as: "What I hear you saying is," or "What are your thoughts?"

Tip: If you're not using a pre-listing package and a proven listing presentation, you *should* be insecure and fidgety. Take care of that before you worry about the rest.

9. Upgrade everything. Your confidence can be affected by many things that can be improved with just a bit of upgrading. Your wardrobe, your spelling, your teeth, your makeup, your speech, your friends, your car, your neighborhood, your hair, your glasses, your office, your accent, your attitude, your real estate signs. Do they have 1800Homehotline.com, as well as a clear, weatherproof home brochure box? Upgrade everything.

Tip: Don't take half measures in correcting the above items. You'll end up spending more time and money in the long run. Make a list of items that cause you any level of insecurity and add them to your goals list. Remember, goals are measurable, specific, time-dependent, and posted, so if you need to upgrade your car, identify what it's going to be, by when you'll have it, and what you need to do to pay for it.

10. Make eye contact. Take this quick test. Are you nervously looking around you seeing who else is in the room, what else is going on or what kind of art they have on the wall? If so, you have an eye contact issue. How do you fix it? Be absolutely fascinated by your prospects and clients. Make them feel like they're the most interesting, most special people you've ever had the pleasure of meeting. Make it all about them by asking questions, but be certain to actually listen to the answers.

A great listing presentation is more about getting to the know the prospects, their motivation, timeframe, and sensibilities and less about slamming them into a cookie-cutter generic presentation. Great eye contact reinforces your interest in the client and their situation, thus, your mission of being of service to them becomes sincere and believable. Risk failure to succeed. It's better to go on appointments with prospects and learn than not to take the appointment at all. (Within reason, after prequalifying, of course!)

When you're learning to become a great listing agent, (or a great anything else for that matter,) it's part of the process to fail. In Part II, there is a typical listing agent timeline. A step-by-step analysis after hundreds of thousands of coaching calls. Each step requires you to increase your skill level. Here's what we see: In the beginning, you're a buyer's agent almost exclusively. Buyers are more excited, more fun, and require less accountability. Your friends and family virtually close themselves if you find something decent to sell them. You believe at this stage that business is easy.

Eventually, however, you run out of buyers. Now, you start having to work with people you don't know, perhaps by means of open house buyers, referrals, or by other ways. Prospecting and lead follow-up becomes necessary and the business is getting harder. In the next stage, you "get screwed" by buyers. They either don't buy at all, don't buy with you, or have major unforeseen deal-wrecking financing or inspection issues. You discover pre-qualification scripts and buyer agency. Now your eyes are open to the possibility that this might require a higher level of skill. You consider getting a coach.

Next, you now start to think about the possibility of being a listing agent or a listing agent at a new level. You list what you can with the skill you have gained so far. Listings are few and far between for the most part. You usually do some sort of deal to make sure that you get and keep the business. Pricing, seller relationships, time management, and negotiating are all harder than you thought. You're making a living, but it's feast or famine. You think, *Surely there's a better way.*

Now you must take your business seriously. You've reached a level of frustration and stagnation, and you no longer seem to be improving. You hire a coach to work on scripts, skills, pre-listing package presentation, objection handling, and closing skills. If you're coachable and willing to face your fears, you can break through those fears by increasing both your skills and accountability. You will have made a major leap. If you don't, you'll fall back into your old undesirable habits.

Charles Stanley, pastor and author, points out: "Fear stifles our thinking and actions. It creates indecisiveness that results in stagnation. I have known talented people who procrastinate indefinitely rather than risk failure. Lost opportunities cause erosion of confidence, and the downward spiral begins."

Always be closing: ABC. Our coaches have found that by being tough on agents at this point, they see an increase of 30-50 percent in appointments set, contracts written, and deals closed. Here's what they all say: Just ask for the business.

Part II

Once you have developed listings, you need to develop a listing system. All great listing agents have a specific system to which they adhere. It doesn't matter if your next listing is your mom's house or a hard-won appointment with an unrepresented seller, otherwise known as a for sale by owner, (FSBO); you operate the same way every time. This allows you to have greater efficiency and speed so that you can handle more appointments, more listings and more closings, all at the same time, without becoming unglued.

Here's the 7-Step Listing Process in chronological order:

1. Generate the lead first. We can stop right here. If you haven't done number one, the rest of it doesn't matter, so get help if you are stymied by generating leads.

2. Urgently follow up on the lead with the intent of setting an appointment.

3. Prequalify for the timeframe, motivation, agent relationships, and price expectations.

4. Send your pre-listing package.

5. Call to confirm the appointment. Arrive five minutes early.

6. Use your polished and proven listing presentation. In our coaching program, we call this the proven home-selling system.

7. Take a listing at the time of the appointment, or as the result of your professional follow up.

8. Lather, rinse, repeat!

Next, we're going to talk about your pre-listing prayer or creed — your pre-listing routine. This is as critical as the listing presentation itself. Taking the listing requires being prepared, skill, and the proper mindset. Your pre-listing mindset is of the utmost importance. You need to adopt your own pre-listing creed or prayer. Below are two examples. Both are very powerful and inspirational.

Stepping aside from real estate for a moment, consider the creed of the United States Marine Corps, written shortly after the attack on Pearl Harbor by USMC Brigadier General William H. Rupertus, who at the time, was the commander of the marine base at San Diego. His intent was to make his men understand that their rifle meant their life, wherever in service they might be. Every Marine is trained, first and foremost, as a rifleman.

It's commonly known as the Rifleman's Creed, but it has also been called *My Rifle, The Creed of the United States Marine*. Every Marine is required to memorize it, and every Marine must live by it. The following is an excerpt:

"This is my rifle. There are many like it, but this one is mine… It is my life. I must master it as I must master my life. My rifle, without me, is useless. Without my rifle, I am useless. I must fire my rifle true. I must shoot straighter than the enemy who is trying to kill me. I must shoot him before he shoots me. I will… My rifle and myself know that what counts in war is not the rounds we fire, the noise of our burst, or the smoke we make. We know that it is the hits that count. We will hit… My rifle is human even as I, because it is my life. Thus, I will learn it as a brother. I will learn its weaknesses, its strength, its parts, its accessories, its sight and its barrel… I will keep my rifle clean and ready. We will become part of each other… Before God, I swear this creed. My rifle and myself are the defenders of my country. We are the masters of our enemy. We are the saviors of my life. So be it, until victory is America's, and there is no enemy, but peace!"

Pastor and author Joel Osteen, uses another positive and powerful short prayer to open each of his messages. "This is my Bible. I am what it says I am. I have what it says I have. I can do what it says I can do. Today I will be taught the word of God. I boldly confess. My mind is alert. My heart is receptive. I'll never be the same. In Jesus' name. God bless you."

It's up to you to adopt a pre-listing prayer or creed to attune your mindset before you ring the next doorbell. Here's our suggested pre-listing prayer or creed. "This is my listing presentation. It shows that I am of service, here to help this homeowner accomplish his goals. I am well-prepared, and today I will ask caring questions and listen to the answers. I will show that I have what it takes to be the highest agent for this task. This homeowner will like and trust me. I am grateful to be here. I am ready to do my job at the highest level possible. I will not leave without a commitment. This is my next listing."

It's time now to follow some strict coaching regarding your listing systems rules now that you get it. Let's review it piece by piece and apply the rules.

Harris Listing Rules

1. Identify, study, polish and perfect at least five specific spokes or pipelines of business as discussed in the previous chapter. Know where your business comes from and how to track your lead-generation. Monitor the effectiveness of what you're doing, and change course with your market's expectations. Remember, if you choose to work exclusively with people who you know versus prospecting folks, such as unrepresented sellers, probate leads or expireds, you'll need to do more work more frequently to generate the leads that you need.

2. Be the fastest, most professional agent possible with regard to furiously fast lead follow-up. You will live or die by how well you

follow-up. 90% of the time the agent who gets the relationship (thus sale) is the agent who speaks with the client first. Seriously, its that simple. Be first. You must always practice "furiously fast lead follow-up." That means every lead is called back within 3 minutes. Our studies prove that if you wait more than 3 minutes you have waited too long. This applies to all leads - if someone emails, texts, messages - the only form of acceptable reply communication is a call. Rule: Furiously fast lead follow-up means calling back within 3 minutes Rule: Always call.

3. Prequalify both buyers and sellers using our proven pre-qualification script. Prequalify for motivation, timeframe, realistic expectations and geographic needs.

4. Our pre-listing package (PLP) will do most of the "selling" for you. Literally our PLP will pre-sell the seller for you. It gives you the competitive advantage of handling the standard objections before you arrive at your appointment and pre-sells you as being the right agent for the job. This shows that you're the most professional of anyone they're interviewing, and it shortens your appointment. That's good for you and for them. It also increases the likelihood of you taking the listing on the spot.

5. Present at the highest level. This means following the listing system that we've provided. The listing appointment is showtime. It's time for you to shine, to be of service, and to show that you are clearly the best at your game. It's not acceptable to go on four appointments and only expect to list two of them. That's failing.

6. Negotiate in such a way that you're honoring your commitment to your client without wrecking the deal in the process. Negotiating is bringing two parties together to create an acceptable outcome for both. It's not bludgeoning the other side, or as some agents say,

making them bleed or making them pay. Taking two people and bringing them to a reasonable outcome is your goal.

7. Lather, rinse, repeat! Go back to point number one, which is generating the lead in the first place.

CHAPTER 8

The Daily Success Game

RULE #8: Done Is Better Than Perfect!

We've covered quite a bit of material so far in the book. What is an agent to do with all this knowledge? Knowledge is of little use without implementation. In this respect, simplification of implementation is the answer. Steve Jobs said something once that has become one of my mantras. "Focus and simplicity. Simple can be harder than complex: You have to work hard to get your thinking clean to make it simple. But it's worth it in the end, because once you get there you can move mountains."

You now should be clear on the actions and the rules necessary to achieve your goals, using real estate as your method of choice to get there. Resist the temptation to over-engineer or over-complicate and overthink what happens next. It's time to act. Many agents never take action because they are afraid that whatever they are doing is not going to be perfect; the prospecting, the listing presentation, the lead follow-up. German Nobel Laureate Thomas Mann summed this point up particularly well: "Order and simplification are the first steps towards the mastery of a subject." Want to master your business? Do it! Even when it's not yet perfect.

For illustrative purposes, let's assume that you are in a reality TV show and I was the host. The show is called, *The Real Estate Success Game.* Here's how the game is played: There are ten agents playing, and it's the final round. Only the most coachable agents have reached this level. You're playing to win the most points in 30 work days. The one with the most points at the end wins a million dollars, tax free. Worth playing, right? You can even play the game again after you win, the only thing that disqualifies a player is losing his or her real estate license. The only rules are that you can and must score points using the list of daily activities that leads you to income in your real estate practice. The goal is to score 50 points daily and you can mix and match activities, repeat a favorite activity, or choose to try something new each day, but each action must be on the list.

During the game, to make it more challenging and interesting for our TV audience, there will be obstacles placed in your way. Sometimes daily, sometimes weekly, even hourly hiccups that can get you off your game and cost you points. What are your potential landmines laying between you and the check for a million bucks? The game creators know that a reliable distraction is your email. Therefore, you'll be repeatedly emailed offers to sign up for easy points-generating solutions. The game show producers also know that some of the players can be distracted for hours following on people on Facebook, Twitter, or other social media outlets.

A player may be required to go to a few extra office meetings to see if he or she can manage time. There's always a possibility of your deals unraveling. The winner is the one who can manage all of the distractions and still score enough points to outscore his competition. This is how you implement what you've learned so far in this book. Stop taking everything so seriously and overthinking it. When you look at it like it's a game, several things will occur.

First, you'll stop thinking that a couple hours a day of productivity will achieve your goals. Second, you'll end the getting-ready-to-get-started-to- someday-be-ready-to-get-to-work syndrome. You'll drill down and focus on only the activities that make a difference. You'll miraculously prequalify your prospects with urgency and skill like you've never known before. And after ten to twenty days on the success game, the business will somehow seem to flow easier. Beware that this may catapult you into new time management challenges, but you'll be making more money in the process. You can always break from the game, hit pause on your mental screen, and re-enter the game when you've gotten a grip again.

So, let's take a closer look at the game and how you can play to win. Your daily goal is to earn at least 50 points. The accumulation of real work in real estate is what leads to consistent, predictable income. Remember, you have only "worked" in real estate when you've scored at least 50 points each day. Each item is worth five points; you can mix and match, you can repeat a particular activity, or earn five points at a time. Do it again and you've earned ten points. For example, you don't have to complete the same actions every day. This list is what actually creates income for you and your family and helps you achieve or even surpass your goals which you set earlier in this book.

What's on the list? We've got obvious things, but at the top is to take a listing. We've got to sign a buyer to buyer agencies, sell a listing, and put a buyer in contract. You can see how these things are making you money. Prequalifying a seller or a buyer prospect, setting a new listing appointment, and calling back 100% of your leads are all worth five points apiece. Talk to five past clients, talk to five people from your center of influence. Five assent managers, get assured sale approval, complete five VPOs, attend a center-of-influence event and, in order to score five points, you must add five new contacts to your database. Talk to five expired listings, talk to five FSBOs, send a referral with signed referral documents, receive a referral with signed referral documents, hold a home buying or selling seminar, get a price reduction of 5% or better, and listen to the daily podcast

Each is worth five points. Remember, the goal is to earn 50 points daily. Here is an example. Let's say you sell one of your listings, that's worth five points. On the same day, you prequalify a new buyer, that's worth five points, and if the buyer signs an agency contract, that's five more points. You've already earned 15 points for the day. Next, you complete five VPOs and earn five more points. You'll call back 100 per cent of your leads for five more points, and because you called those leads you'll also get new listing appointment, which is worth five more points. You now have 30 points. I think you'll agree that so far, you've had a very productive day. So, let's get back to work. You decide to work in your existing listing inventory and get two price reductions worth five points apiece. You now have 40, and it's not even time for lunch yet!

When you get back to the office, you call five past clients and earn another five points. You're almost finished for the day. You didn't quite get to 50 points, but look at what you have accomplished by getting to 45. Now it's time to listen to the podcast, and that's your easy last five points! Even if you have zero listings, you can still score 50 points by repeating some of the activities. For example, talking to ten past clients, you'll score ten points. Calling ten expireds is also good for ten points. The idea is to *spend your time on an activity that creates income*. The upshot of this is although you are playing a game, you do get paid for your work. You don't have to pretend that you're in a virtual reality TV show to get to work and earn from your activities. We've just created The Daily Success Game (*see Appendix*) to help you stay on track and to implement all the things we've been talking about so far in the book.

CHAPTER 9

Choose
Your Path

RULE #9: Repetitious Boredom Pays Off

This chapter focuses on creating a scalable business without over-leveraging yourself. Let's drill down even further.

Freedom only comes from the systematic implementation of inspired action. As Tim Harris explains it, "Long-term, ever-increasing success only comes from doing what you don't want to do, when you don't want to do it, at the highest level." Julie Harris adds, "That's why they call it work and not vacation."

What does it mean this mean? Let's conquer the "what you don't want to do" part first. Write down the things that you don't want to do in real estate, don't feel like doing, don't like to do with consistency, avoid like the plague, have sworn off, get panic attacks over, worry about at night. Each agent may have a slightly different list. Realize that these are usually the very things that actually create income in any thriving real estate practice.

Based on hundreds and thousands of coaching calls handled by our operation over the years, here are some observations. The first thing that agents don't like to do is generate leads. Anything that sounds like prospecting or lead-generation. Prospecting requires discipline and marketing money. Paying for leads is an act of desperation with little quality or quantity control. The most important part of your business is often avoided, procrastinated about, misunderstood, or even ignored.

The second thing many avoid is following up on those leads, especially with urgency. Often, agents claim that they don't have enough leads, but when we dig deeper, it's almost always discovered that the real issue is a lack of professional lead follow-up urgency. It's avoided due to not knowing what to say, or not wanting to sound pushy, like a sales person, or simply from laziness. We've seen a 30 to 40 percent increase in gross commission income for our agents who follow the 18 Lead Follow-up Rules.

Prequalifying is another aspect some avoid. This is sometimes because of ignorance, not knowing how critical this step is and what the liability is when it isn't done. Sometimes, it's understood but avoided because the agent doesn't want to risk hearing something that he or she doesn't know, or simply wants to avoid hearing the word "no." This demonstrates a lack of business maturity. Both reasons get cured when you have a terrible experience that could have been avoided if you had just pre-qualified.

Presenting is a fourth area some procrastinate on. Why use a listing presentation when you can just get away with your personality most of the time? Unfortunately, most of the time doesn't create predictable, scalable results. Using a proven method to always take to the listing is the only way.

The next area on our list is negotiating. You may not want to do this, but in this case, you must. There are two common issues here. One is drama and two is procrastination. Learn to be a great negotiator.

Closing is next: both closing the deal and closing for the appointment. Agents don't close because they don't want rejection, and because they don't have the scripts to do it. You'll notice our list of those things that "you don't want to do" has to do with making money, and all are critical, skill-based items. Let's move on to the "when you don't want to do it" part and deal with that.

It goes without saying that no one wants to do what they don't want to do, ever, at any time. Accept the fact that you're never going to feel like doing certain aspects of the job. Ever. That's the first step. So, stop waiting to have the desire suddenly, like everything is okay. What do you do about this? You must determine when you are your most productive. Not everyone is a morning person. Everyone asks, when is the best time to prospect or do lead follow-up? Well, the answer is to do it when you are at your best. If you're super-focused after lunch, do it then, but do it regularly as part of your job. If you are a morning person, take advantage of that.

Consider doing your lead follow-up or prospecting on at least one weekday evening and on Saturday morning to capture what we call the "unobtainable" leads, those who are otherwise hard to find. If you keep calling at the same time on the same day, they're going to be at work, so you've got to mix it up, so try a weekday evening or Saturday morning.

Next, ask yourself if you only work when you feel like working, how productive would you actually be? For some of you reading the book right now, that is how you go throughout your life and in your practice. Working in spurts will get you cash flow spurts, versus having a gushing fire hose of business as the result of your consistent efforts. It's called work because it produces results, income, contribution, and satisfaction. Vacation happens as the result of that hard work. Work when it's work hours, and vacation when it's vacation time. The static happens when you're not really committed to either. Now, at the highest level, what does that mean? You've decided to take action. Do what you don't want to do and do it when you don't want to do it, but now we've got to talk about at the highest level.

First, stop dabbling and stop polishing. Take each part of the business. Are you the best at it? Lead-generation. Lead follow-up. Prequalifying, presenting, negotiating, closing. What will it take for you to be the best at those things which are most important? Track your results. Which spokes of your lead-generation wheel are generating the highest number and quality of leads? How many of those leads does it take to set a qualified appointment? How many appointments does it take to generate closed buyer and seller business? Are you all in or not? Are you 100 percent invested and committed to each part of the business? To real estate in general? Or are you trying it out, waiting it out, to see how it goes?

We know from thousands of coaching calls that the agents who are all in and have decided that this is their work, are professional real estate advisors, and they always do better than posers who are "trying it out." It's okay to have another job to sustain your income, of course, as you get going in real estate. We are advocates of that. Mentally, you must be all in and committed, with failure not being an option.

Remember, at 211 degrees water is just hot; one degree more makes it boil. Sometimes that last, best effort, that last degree creates the boiling point in your business. Some of you don't take action because you think it takes too much more action. When in fact, sometimes it is only 1 to 10 degrees more, depending on how skilled you are, how experienced and how motivated you are, to make all the difference in the world. It's that last degree that makes water boil.

Your job now is to implement these things: lead-generation, lead follow-up, prequalifying, presenting, negotiating, and closing. Lather, rinse, repeat. When you get serious about what we just discussed, you'll find your business will temporarily be more challenging simply due to the discipline and the upgraded skill that's required. In the long term, it will be far easier, since you will find that long-term, ever-increasing success and predictable income.

CHAPTER 10

The Six Critical Things

RULE #10: Be the Best at What Matters

Eric Schmidt, former CEO of Google, was giving advice to Sergey Brin, the new CEO of Google. Schmidt told him to "be great at five things." In Steve Job's autobiography, he tells that he received similar advice from both his father and his mentors. We agree with them both. Being great at a simple list of things is what will bring you wealth in real estate. In a world of distractions, how do know what to do in real estate that definitely leads to a pay check? Is it your website, networking, paying for leads, or tweaking your landing page? You're probably busy enough just holding deals together.

What's an agent to do? Keep it simple. Become great at lead-generation, lead follow-up, prequalifying, presenting, negotiating and closing. When you're the best at each of these six critical things, it will be impossible for you not to meet or exceed your financial goals.

Lead generation rules:

1. Maintain a minimum number of buyers and listings, always. Listings are more important. This is your number one job in real estate. 2. Know where you get your leads.

3. What are your spokes? Past clients, centers of influence, referrals, builders, open houses, unrepresented sellers otherwise known as FSBOs, expired listings, and withdrawns. The list goes on, but choose your sources and become the best at generating leads from them. Some of our clients are best at open houses. They have figured out not just how to hold an open house on Sunday, but how to monetize that open house. If you claim that your business comes from for sale by owners, be the best at the for sale by owners.

4. Following a daily schedule that focuses on generating new business is critically important. It's a decision that you must make every day. Make a commitment to stop dabbling, trying out, messing around with, or seeing how it goes. Be the best at it. Decide that it does work, because you're working it.

Lead Follow-up Rules:

1. Follow up on 100% of your leads daily, regardless of the lead source, without regard to anything else with which you are dealing. No exceptions. Remember leads have no value. Prequalified have-to seller leads have value.

2. Follow up with the tightest possible urgency. Leads, unlike some wines, do not get better with age, so shoot for three minutes or less. (Unless you're on an actual listing appointment.) It should go without saying, follow up relentlessly. Call until they list or buy with you, list or buy with someone else, tell you they'll never list or buy, or get a restraining order against you because you're so relentless. (We're kidding about the restraining order!)

3. Use scripts in your follow-ups (*see Appendix*). Use compelling messages that make them want to call you back. Just saying, "Hey, how's it going? Give me a call when you're ready," is not an example of a compelling lead follow-up script. When you call, and say, "I

have those numbers you asked for the last time we spoke. Call me, because I can meet with you at 6 o'clock tonight or Saturday morning at 10:00," is much better.

4. Get rid of elaborate follow-up requirements, such as only emailing them because they emailed you, or not leaving messages for invalid reasons. The only follow-up is follow-up with urgency, by phone or in person.

Prequalifying Rules:

1. Prequalify 100% of the time, including repeat and referral leads. Prequalify your best friend the same as you would a cold lead.

2. Prequalify for motivation and for timeframe.

3. Use prequalifying scripts for both buyers and sellers. Never go on a listing presentation without knowing the answers to the following: Are they speaking with other agents? What price do they have in mind? Why are they selling, and what is their timeframe? Again, those are your seller basic four points. You should never go on the appointment if you don't know those things.

Presentation Rules:

1. Have real buyer and listing presentations. Make sure they're powerful and proven. What does that point mean? Not just by phone, not over Facebook. Have real presentations.

2. Create and use a pre-listing presentation. Make sure it's powerful and proven. If you don't have a powerful, proven listing presentation, contact us at www.timandjulieharris.com and learn how you can get access to ours!

3. Know your scripts, objection-handlers and closes.

4. Develop a high level of versatility and skills so that you're not just working with people who are just like you, who fall into your lap, or who are referred to you.

5. Learn how to close, to reduce losing potential clients and wasting time on endless follow-up.

Negotiating Rules:

1. Understand that negotiating means bringing two parties together to reach a mutual agreement, plain and simple. Not beating on the other side, making them cry, making the other person bleed, or any of those crazy negotiating things that you read about or hear about.

2. Learn to be in control of your emotions so that you can do the best job for your clients. Be creative and flexible and maintain a mindset of being of service even when the other parties don't behave the way that you desire.

3. Never. Ever. Give up. If you have a buyer who wants to buy and a seller who wants to sell, your job is to figure out how to get them to close.

4. Some money is better than no money. Assess the situation before you say no to deals that you do have the power to close. Don't be part of the problem; be part of the solution.

Closing Rules:

1. Understand that closing is the logical result of a great presentation. If you don't have a great presentation, you'll never be able to close well.

2. Learn how to do soft closes, assumptive closes and direct closes.

3. Close at least five times before you give up. That's probably five more than you're comfortable with.

4. Always use the "Sharpie Close©." To learn more about it, contact us at www.timandjulieharris.com. If you aren't the best in your market at the six critical skills outlined above, hire the best coach today, or become okay with your production. If you already have a coach, do what they are telling you to do. Do your homework. Identify where your weaknesses are in each of the skills above, and create a specific plan to become the best.

CHAPTER 11

The World Is Your Oyster... If You Make It So!

RULE #11: FREEDOM Is Being Self-Employed Every Day, Not Self- Unemployed

Why is real estate the world's greatest opportunity to build wealth? Many people assume that the wealthiest people are famous actors and politicians, or people who were born with wealth, when in fact, the wealthiest people in the world, almost without exception, have been, and still are, sales people. Why is that?

Sales allows the highest level of freedom, with the least obstacles, compared to other fields of practice. Let's examine this, further. First, there's little to no barrier to entry. There's no experience necessary. You are prohibited from getting into real estate unless you've done A, B, and C. There is no apprentice requirement to work for somebody for 20 years before you get your real estate license. That's a blessing and a curse, as many of you know.

There's no investment other than the cost of a license, which usually ranges from $800 to $1500. There is no knowledge required except the four required classes to earn your real estate license. What you need to know can be gained using the "Earn While You Learn" strategy. In fact, one can obtain a real estate license without ever having owned a home.

In the field of real estate, there's no income cap. Nobody's going to tell you that you can't make any more for this job, or to get the next pay raise that you must get an additional degree or you're required to relocate to a place where you don't want to live. You can make as much or as little as you desire in real estate.

Also, there's no geographic requirement to your job. You can live anywhere in the world and make great income in real estate due to the portability of your skills. Yes, you must get licensed somewhere else and you need to learn their local principles and practices, but that isn't terribly time consuming. No geographic requirement is also a huge blessing.

Unlike some other sales jobs, you are not required to purchase the inventory. This was kind of a big revelation when we first realized this. Consider a car dealer. A car dealer has to develop a floor plan and obtain a certain line of credit for a certain number of cars. They have a time restriction for keeping vehicles in the showroom, before they need to turn that inventory over. They're invested in their inventory. That's not so in real estate.

A grocer's inventory has expiration dates. Although real estate listings can expire, and you can lose out to a competitor who then can list that property, it doesn't actually expire like bad bananas.

Another positive factor of real estate sales is that the business is skill-based and isn't determined by influence, social or economic status, or other factors. You really can climb the ladder at your own pace, as long as you have reasonable skill, which is what we're here to provide. It's merit based, and that's a huge blessing.

Your skills are portable to other price ranges, areas, and even services. Sales training applies to many types of sales, and isn't limited to real estate. We have successfully coached people in the area of car sales, car wash chains, and we've even coached people in the behavioral health area. It's all based on the same basic skill set.

The opportunities, even under the real estate umbrella, are multiple. In addition to real estate sales, you can also be a broker, or work in development as a builder, or you can represent builders. You can be a property manager. You can be a flipper. You can work in mortgages, titles, or processing. Real estate is not just one job. In fact, some of the most successful agents work several of these categories. They're in sales, but they're also doing some flips and they manage some property for themselves and other people. This point and our next point is really where the rubber meets the road in our earlier definition of wealth!

An appreciable quality of the real estate business is that it can be easily passed along to future generations. Many of our coaching clients have the specific intent of passing along their business and/or rental property holdings to their offspring, to their partners, or to a member of their team. Additionally, overhead is minimal, as long as you manage it correctly. You can make millions paying thousands or less. You don't have to spend everything that you make despite of what some people around you may be doing.

Next, there's no space required. Returning to the car dealer analogy, if you have to accommodate car inventory, you have to keep them somewhere, which means you're leasing property. You've got to store your stuff someplace. In real estate, overhead is minimal and hardly any space is required. You just need a place to hang your license.

Consider the expensive malpractice insurance that doctors and attorneys are required to carry. Real estate professionals have minimum insurance requirements, which are normally carried by your broker, your E&O, (errors and omissions) insurance. Licensing requirements are comparatively minimal considering the money to be made. Even continuing education requirements are not as demanding as they are in many other professions.

Recognize that the area of real estate is the greatest opportunity in the world for the best wealth building strategy for yourself, for your family, and for creating the life of your dreams.

CHAPTER 12

Choose
Your Path

RULE #12: FOCUS: F.ollow O.ne C.ourse U.ntil S.uccessful

Yes, you actually can control much of your real estate practice. It's best to start with the end in mind. There are five major paths which have definitive characteristics. Which path you choose should be determined by your personal situation. Consider the numbers and goals you worked out in our earlier exercises. Knowing your numbers and using the Real Estate Treasure Map allows you to really drill down on this.

Now, we'll take a look at each type of agent, so you can see the different paths to success. We'll look at five different criteria for each type. We'll compare and contrast the income potential, the speed limit of the business, the time commitment, the growth and net, and even examine the lifestyle of each. You'll get a feel for the pluses and minuses of each path.

First, we'll start with the basic assistant or transaction coordinator. In this role, ideally, you are licensed. It's possible to be an assistant or a transaction coordinator without a license, but we don't recommend it for legal and logistical reasons. Let's assume that you're licensed. The income usually ranges from $10 to $15 per hour for an assistant and

$250 to $450 per closed transaction, as a transaction coordinator (TC). Some TCs are paid both hourly and per transaction. There are several iterations of this role, but generally $25,000 to $50,000 per year is about what you can expect.

Generally, your growth and net aren't that different. Just pay your taxes off the top, and you're left with the rest. The benefit of being in this position is that you're a licensed and "in real estate," but you don't have a specific job, a salary, or predictable income and virtually no expense. You don't have to worry about regeneration, competing for listings, driving buyers around, or any of the other responsibilities of the independent agent.

The downside of this role is your income cap. This is a job, not a business. For some agents, that's completely appropriate for their needs, and to their schedule constraints. Many of our top agents started out in this position while their kids were young or while they were working another job in the evening. It's a great way to learn the business, and a great way to be in the business. The time commitment is the most predictable of all of our agent types. For the most part, you'll be working 30 to 40 hours per week and will work during normal business hours when mortgage, title, and inspection companies are open. As with all of our profiles, you can choose to commit to this path or simply use it as a stepping stone to the next level.

The single agent is the next type of agent. As a single agent, there are many factors that can affect your potential income, your lifestyle, and your time management. Most of these items are in your control. You'll need to consider the following: your available time to work in real estate, family time, other jobs, and other commitments that have to be considered. Consider the areas in which you wish to sell. Do your research. The suburb or the ZIP code in which you live may or may not be a good choice to pursue. Use your MLS to research which areas are selling the most homes and have the lowest days on the market. What's hot and what's not. Determine the quality brokerages available for you to join. Ideally, you'll want to be with a brand name brokerage, the one with the most market share in the area that you wish to sell.

Why is this? The objection *I've never heard of you or your company, why should I consider listing with you* doesn't go away. Count on hearing it. That objection will occur on virtually every appointment, unless you're only going to work with personal referrals.

Consider also the average sale price in the area where you wish to work. All of the above questions must be considered by the independent solo agent. These are factors which affect everything you do in this role. Your potential income depends on a reasonable average sale price. Work in an area that actually has sales occurring, and be certain to have the time available to pursue the business necessary to drive your income. It's an interconnected web.

You'll need to use your Real Estate Treasure Map to determine your own specific numbers. Take your basic monthly overhead requirements and divide by the potential net commissions to you, and determine how many units you must sell to meet those basic needs. Do the math a second time once you've completed the goals and you know what it would take to create the lifestyle of your dreams. Again, it's usually about three times what it takes to pay for your basic overhead. Using the treasure map, you'll determine how many listings you need at all times to create that income.

CHAPTER 13

Ready for Take-off?

RULE #13: Don't Keep Circling the Runway

What is the true income potential as an individual agent? Again, this depends greatly on the average sell price in your area, the commission split you have with your broker, and the time you have to commit. That said, we have coached many solo agents who have grossed up to $1 million yearly with only a transaction coordinator on their team. More commonly, the single-agent scenario replaces the agent's previous income. That's what we hear all the time.

Interesting fact. The most profitable agents neting 50%+ have no more than 2-3 assistants. Big teams net less than 10%!

"I'm in real estate, so I can get out of my old job. I want replace it." Then typically, they'll either stay there or increase it. Assuming you follow our specific plans and are coachable, the single agent can certainly expect to make over $100,000 annually. It's common to reach $250,000 or more before any significant personnel is required, other than the transaction coordinator and perhaps a part-time assistant. This is a great career and can have the best net income situation, without the hassle of managing a team, and buying leads to feed a buyer-agent machine.

The biggest challenge a solo agent faces is time management. The speed limit is different for everyone, but it's a real phenomenon. The solo agent can only work with so many buyers at once before running out of time and energy. Working with buyers is physical energy; working with listings is mental energy. This brings up the lifestyle issue. It's critical to understand what we call the airplane analogy. When does a plane use the most fuel? During takeoff, cruising altitude or landing?

Takeoff, of course. We've all experienced what it feels like to have those jet engines fire up. The plane shakes. It's loud. You feel the force of the power lifting the plane up. Once you get to cruising altitude, it levels out. The pilots use the autopilot, and it's smooth sailing from there. That's when you see the pilot leave the cockpit to use the restroom, and you wonder who's flying the thing! It's because he's relying on his copilot and the autopilot.

Your real estate trajectory is similar to that jet. In the beginning, you use lots of fuel; tons of energy. That's because the first few years, are so fraught with challenges, cruising altitude is often never achieved. Some agents never get past a few thousand feet. They keep trying to take off, and in some cases, they keep circling the runway, never getting past the deal-to-deal lifestyle.

When you become a listing agent, figuring out your magic number — the number of listings required for you to maintain at all times to fuel your consistent income stream — that's cruising altitude. Not being a listing agent will help keep you in perpetual takeoff mode. As a listing agent, you have far more choices about how to run your practice. You may choose to achieve and maintain a certain income level based on your magic number of listings and never hire additional team members. You may decide to double or triple your magic number, taking your income to the next level, by leveraging your time with people and technology. You have choices as the listing agent that you don't have as a buyer's agent.

Let's be clear here. We're not talking about being able to just handle listings. Many agents can handle listings. They take listings by referral, by chance, but primarily make their living with buyers.

Being a listing agent means the following. You follow a specific listing system. You prequalify all listing leads using your proven seller prequalification script. You use your proven pre-listing package every time in every situation. You use your proven listing presentation every time and are taking at least 90% of the listings for which you interview, regardless if you are competing or not. You're excellent at handling objections. You can take any listing, in any price range, in any neighborhood, due to your systematic and proven practices. That's what being a listing agent means.

Your speed limit is determined simply by how many listings you can get and maintain at all times. Being systematized and organized, following a schedule, you should be able to manage at least 20 listings by yourself. The nature of your listings can affect this, but generally between 20 and 30 listings requires a part-time listing assistant. If most of your listings are in the same kind of building, for example, or you're handling a new construction neighborhood, of course, you can manage more, due to the economics of scale. Usually, however, above 20 listings are different sellers. Your time management will be affected by the number of relationships that you must manage. We recommend that our coaching clients utilize the seller's 12-week communication plan to systematize listing maintenance, achieve price reductions when necessary, and to foster repeat and referral business.

Next, we're going to turn attention to the new agent, the newer agent, the I-feel-like-a-new-agent, the struggling agent, or the returning agent massive action plan. If you're any of the listed above, you're most likely a single-agent practitioner. Or you maybe just feel like you're in that situation, struggling, returning, or in need of an action plan. Anyone who feels an experience deficit, or not up to date with regard to technology, this plan is designed to fast-forward you into profit.

Remember, that for all agents, knowledge equals confidence and ignorance equals fear.

Fast Launch or Re-launch Plan

1. Complete your required post-licensing CE credit before it's too late. If you haven't done it yet, take either an appraisal or contracts class.

2. Take an MLS class at your local board. Every MLS system is more robust and has a lot more functionality than what you learn from your broker or manager. This is going to help you with your comparative market analysis research, your CMAs, as well as searches for property for buyers. You'll be able to enter your listings faster and more accurately. They're going look better in the MLS, which will attract more showings for you. If you don't know how to use your MLS, you'll never do any of that. This applies to both the new or returning agent, but certainly for single-agent practitioners. If you're running a team, you can use this checklist to fold in your newest team members.

3. Take a contracts class from your board of realtors or from your brokerage. It's not worth risking your license over rookie mistakes. Also, any time your contracts change, which has become frequent lately with new laws and regulations, do take the classes offered. Lots of boards require this, so make sure you do it.

4. Attend a buyer closing. This seems simple, but many of you, especially west of the middle the country, don't have any idea what happens with a closing. Take notes and ask questions of the closer after the buyer leaves. When a buyer asks you what to take to closing, how to prepare, what to expect, you'll know. Be able to prepare an accurate estimate of buyer's net sheet.

5. Attend a seller closing. Take notes, ask questions after the seller leaves. When your sellers ask you what to expect, what to bring to closing, how long it will take, and what happens there, you'll know. Be able to prepare an estimated seller's net sheet. That is the conglomeration of all of their costs, which they do expect you to know something about.

6. Attend a buyer's loan application and ask the lender for a checklist. Buyers are given this prior to the loan application. You should know what's required to complete the process. What's the typical timeframe that a buyer can expect for approval? What's underwriting? How do ratios and credit affect buyer's approval? Have the following lender relationships with different types of lenders: FHA and a VA lender, which is usually also great with first-time buyers, a traditional 20-percent-down A-paper lender, and a jumbo loan lender. Some of you need agricultural or farm lenders. Hard money lenders. You should probably know something about SBA, Small Business Association, lender possibilities as well.

7. Tour 10 homes in each price segment of your market. This is very important for nearly everyone in any iteration of real estate. Get to know your market. Go from the lowest to the highest. The more you know, the more you'll earn. Expand your geographic knowledge as you do that tour of 10 homes in each price range. That way, you're not referring things that you shouldn't refer. You're not calling people back because you've never heard of the ZIP Code.

8. Use your MLS to determine which ZIP Codes in your county or city are selling the fastest, with the most volume, what's hot and what's not. Update this knowledge quarterly, if not monthly.

9. Tour new construction if your area has it. You will probably not find this in your MLS, so look in your local paper, search online, tour all price ranges and keep a new construction file so you know who's building what and where. Often, builders will have special promotions. We've seen cases where they pay 5% commissions to

the buyer side and a listing agent or they don't have a listing agent. There's lots of creative promotions. They have bonuses if things are closed by a certain date. Know your new construction.

10. Use whiteboards for visual accountability, so you can track where you are today versus where you need to be to meet or exceed your goals.

11. Use the 18 relentless follow-up rules (*see Appendix*).

12. Decide which three lead-generation spokes you will pursue first if you are a newer agent, and which ones you will polish if you're an experienced agent. Listen to all of our coaching scripts and podcasts on those topics at www.timandjulieharris.com

13. Complete your pre-listing package after listening to all of the coaching in the section. Don't reinvent the wheel. Just follow our very specific examples, format and coaching on those.

14. Complete your real estate treasure map. That is your business plan. That gives you your big-picture business plan.

15. Follow the survival plan, short term, whether you've been in real estate forever, or you are just freshly licensed. Follow the survival plan typically for 60 to 90 days until you have at least three pending transactions, then convert over to your treasure map or the 90-day massive action plan.

16. Set up three bank accounts. One for operations where you pay your business bills; one for savings, save at least 5 per cent from every check; and one for taxes, ideally saving 20 per cent off of every check. Remember, at least 25 per cent, which is part savings and part taxes off your net commission, really doesn't belong to you. Set it aside for taxes and savings. Don't start out by getting behind.

Here are the rules of this plan.

1. Don't skip steps. Each step in this plan is designed to get you into knowledge and out of ignorance. Each step is both practical and applicable. You can do 100% of these items without spending much money. Your CE class and training classes might cost something, but aside from that, this is inexpensive, if not free, education.

2. Don't listen to any agents, coaches, trainers, brokers or advisers who aren't at least as successful as you intend to be. If you are considering hiring a coach use compareacoach.com. You will be stunned to learn many real estate coaches never sold real estate! They are not qualified to advise you. Everyone will be trying to give you advice. Many will try to convince you that you're not supposed to make any real income for the first year or that feast and famine is the typical agent's lifestyle. Don't buy it. Their advice is influenced by their inexperience, which may or may not have anything to do with you, your motivation, your action plan, your education or your mindset. Insulate yourself from opinions.

3. Take massive action daily. Spend 75% of your day in lead-generation, 10% on education and 15% on actual appointments. Most agents spend most the day getting ready to get started to possibly take action at a later date. Your number one job in real estate is to generate leads. Nothing else matters if you're leadless.

4. Don't spend money that you don't have. Make the pledge not to charge unnecessary, unproven speculative items to your credit cards. The following four black holes of expenditure are off-limits to you: buying leads, branding, marketing, and farming.

5. Do you make sure you're with the right broker. It's disruptive and costly to move brokerages, especially multiple times. Interview with several and understand their benefits, the market share, reputation, commission schedule and culture. Make an informed decision and

stick with it for at least a year. If you do have to make a switch, do it between Christmas and New Year's to minimize disruption of your cash flow and your momentum.

6. Of course, listen to our daily podcast, Real Estate Coaching Radio, which you can find on iTunes, Stitcher and more. We will be your primary mastermind adviser, educator and advocate.

7. Get in the habit of earning money versus burning money. No matter where you are in your career and in your trajectory, earning is better than burning.

Part III

What is the true income potential of an individual agent? Again, this depends greatly on the average sale price in your area, the commission split price you have with your broker, and the time you commit to the business. That said, we have coached and known many solo agents who have grossed up to a million dollars yearly using only a transaction coordinator and a part-time personal assistant. Fact: The most profitable agents are listing agents with small teams. Most teams (let alone big teams) make less that 10% before tax profit. More commonly, the single-agent scenario replaces the agent's previous income, assuming you follow our specific plans and are coachable. The solo agent can certainly expect to make over a $100,000 annually, and it's common to reach $250,000 or more before any significant personnel is required other than the transaction coordinator and possibly a part-time assistant.

This is a great career and can have the best net income situation without the hassle of managing a team, having pressure to buy leads to feed an army of buyer agents, or other major expenses required to fuel a bigger machine. Positive factors for the solo agent include a higher net, less expenses, and the ability to be a home office agent and be accountable primarily only to yourself and to your family. Negatives really get down to what you can personally handle before you hit your own speed limit. Some agents we've coached get unglued with three deals pending at once and a few active sellers, but our top producing solo agents can handle a lot more, up to 30 listings at once and 6-8 pendings at all times. A few of them have handled more than that, but much of this ability we attribute to the application of technology and systems, experience, character and personality.

Critical requirements for the solo agent to reach cruising altitude and manage more transactions, in less time, with diminished stress, include the following rules:

1. Have a business plan and follow it. The Real Estate Treasure Map is the all-encompassing introspective tool that won't let you down. Go to freecoachingcallsforagents.com to download your free treasure map.

2. For the every agent, use your pre-listing package before each and every appointment, even if you think it's a slam dunk.

3. Have a polished listing presentation and buyer presentation every time.

4. Solo agents, communicate with all active listing clients every week at a specific time, with a specific format to the call. Use the seller's 12 week communication plan to stay on track.

5. Develop, polish, and maintain at least five strong spokes in your lead- generation wheel. If one stops working, find out why and consider replacing it with a new spoke.

6. Eliminate ego; it serves no purpose in your business. We recommend the book Ego is the Enemy, by Ryan Hartman to help in this area.

7. Use whiteboards and visual accountability to track your leads, listings, buyers, pendings, and closed transactions.

8. Use a transaction coordinator. You'll make more than you'll spend on a transaction coordinator, have them do the hourly wage type work.

9. Monitor your market closely; take what it's willing to give you. If you suddenly see tons of new construction, learn about new construction. If your ZIP code that used to be hot becomes "not,"

be willing to change your ways. Versatile agents always make the highest incomes.

10. Spend your time only in the most important areas, being careful to avoid pretty, shiny things that promise to eliminate your lead-generation responsibilities. Your number one job is to generate business.

CHAPTER 14

The Not-Lazy Way To Find New Listings

RULE #14: The Future Belongs To The Furiously Fast

It's time to address some common mistakes we frequently observe about Realtors®. First, we see passivity in the process. Don't wait for the buyer to email you what they want. It's not their job to find the right home. It's what they hired you to do. Are you looking daily for homes that meet the buyer's needs? Do they know that you're not? Wouldn't they fire you if they knew you weren't even bothering to look for them?

Second, we see a lack of urgency. Be the first to see new inventory, monitor your hot sheet and be ready to pounce.

The last oversight that we see is the failure of some agents to recognize that not all homes are sold through the MLS. Know where else they come from. There's an NAR statistic that indicates that as many as 30 percent of sales, particularly in places like Northern California, are now pocket listings, meaning they never hit the MLS.

So, how does one create inventory when it seems like there isn't anything to sell? One of the most common complaints we hear, or requests that we get from coaching clients is, "I've got all these great buyers. I could be making tons of money and helping a lot of people, but I just can't find them anything to buy." Now, if you're blessed to be in a market where you have plenty to choose from, maybe this isn't for you, but you will eventually come across this issue. Where do we find inventory that's not in the MLS?

There are several approaches to finding "nonexistent" inventory and creating listing opportunities for yourself. Don't choose just one or two of these, do all of them:

Note: Become a listing agent asap and consider referring your buyer leads to other agents for 25-30%. Keep only the sellers who are listed with you and will buy.

1. New construction. This is probably my favorite approach. New construction is almost never listed in the MLS. Find what's being built by looking in your local weekend newspaper and actually visiting all the models. Start a file called "New Construction" and know the inventory. Know the price range, the area, the spec homes, builder perks, and special financing. Become friends with the new build reps. They can be a great source of resell referrals.

2. Communicate regularly with your own past clients and center-of-influence contacts so that you have your own pocket listings. Those are your personal shadow inventory. Offer free CMAs, (Comparative Market Analysis), for purposes of property tax assessment revisions.

3. Wanted ads for your well qualified, highly motivated buyers. Run specific ads, describing their needs and targeting the exact neighborhoods they're looking for (see Appendix).

4. Use Zillow.com, "Make Me Move." These are homeowners who have gone to Zillow, created their home's profile, updated the information, and actually stated the price they want. Before you criticize their higher price (because it almost always is) realize that their stated price might be what they owe, or maybe they're a great short sale candidate, or maybe they just don't know how to price their home. Use printerbees.com door hangers, postcards, or simply door knock those prospects from Zillow.

5. Use Zillow again for free pre-foreclosure information. These are exact addresses of homeowners who are already in pre-foreclosure, and they're going to have to sell. Sign up for a free account and you'll be able to get the exact address instead of just the street name.

6. Expireds — new ones and old ones. You know that they wanted to sell their home at one point and time, so check the withdrawns as well.

7. For sale by owners; they're crying out for help, with a help wanted sign and a phone number.

8. Improve your personal center of influence in networking so that you are the one with the pocket listings. Use BNI, your Chamber of Commerce, charity events, meetup.com. Go to at least three events per week, so that you are the go-to person for all things real estate.

9. Register with all the referral-fee-only companies like Dignified Transition Solutions, agentmachine.com, and agentpronto.com so that you're an insider like all of our ASD students are.

10. Call "for rent by owners" in your area using the newspaper, Craigslist, and classified ads to find their information. These are probably small investors or people who have already moved, keeping their old house as a rental. Just ask, "Have you considered selling it instead of keeping it as a rental?" These are not in the MLS.

11. Network with agents to be notified of their pocket listings, pre-market REO's.

12. Work with your investors and run ads that say, "We pay cash for homes." Are you really going to pay cash for homes? Maybe you are or your investor is, but you just want your phone to ring with opportunity.

13. Run ads for "move up" type listings. The type of homes that first-time home sellers will move to, so that you can then list the home they're coming from. Borrow other agents' listings if necessary.

14. Utilize 1800homehotline.com in your paper on postcards, door hangers. This works best with want ads, free CMA offers, and with pre-foreclosure prospects to discuss their options.

Tip: Using 800 Home Hotline for your main phone number on any type of marketing will increase your incoming calls exponentially. Agents who use this system usually sell their own listings themselves, have more homes in their own inventory, and do more transactions.

CHAPTER 15

Is Two Always Better Than One?

RULE #15: We Love Teams... *Profitable* Teams

Let's examine a partnership in real estate. Whether that means a married couple or business partners, the structure for success is the same. One of the advantages to the partnership model is that it can take a couple of directions. It merits taking some time to consider what lifestyle you want, particularly if you're a couple who has never worked together before.

Usually these partnerships form when a spouse wants to get away from his or her "normal job," when retired or laid off, or simply wants a change. Alternatively, the partnership comes about when a solo agent reaches his or her cruising altitude, but realizes he or she could possibly be doing more with decreased time, if partnered with someone. It should be emphasized that the partnership model takes hard work to run smoothly. This is not a "set it and forget it" relationship. Different personalities, sell styles, schedules, family situations, and skill levels all will be highlighted as soon as you start working together. Be prepared to be flexible.

Follow our coaching and remember, you're building a business, not just servicing a hobby. What should the goal of the partnership be? Keep in mind that your product is profit. However, there are two approaches one might take. First, you may choose to double your income by doubling your efforts. (This can be done two different ways, which we'll address shortly.)

The second approach to profiting by a partnership, is to keep your income basically the same, or maybe a reasonable level higher, but use your partnership to leverage your time back. First, we'll tackle the idea of doubling your income through doubling your efforts.

The key question to answer here is: Does each partner want to do the core work required to create profit, that's necessary as a solo agent? Will both partners lead-generate, follow-up on leads, prequalify, present to buyers and sellers, negotiate and close? If this is the case, your efficiencies will come from sharing a transaction coordinator, sharing costs, covering for each other on scheduling issues, and sharing office fees. This probably won't result in increased time. Furthermore, in our experience as coaches, it's not that efficient. Conflict frequently arises regarding who does what and with which client.

We recommend that you follow the second model, which is more effective, efficient, and is set up like a real business, with systems, strategies and organization. What are the steps to accomplishing a peaceful, productive, and profitable partnership, where each person is fulfilled financially and still has a life? Many of our grizzled veteran coaching clients come to us with the specific request, "I want to make more money, but also have a life. I want to have time for my kids, or grandkids, travel, and not go crazy."

Let's look at the step-by-step process to build this model. We'll keep it practical and tactical.

The 10 Action Steps for Building a Partnership:

1. Make a list of all of the action items to run your business. Decide which partner will handle each task. Be 100 percent committed to

owning that task, being the best at it, and systematizing. (Use Michael Gerber's book, *The E Myth*, as your guide through this process.)

2. Complete your Real Estate Treasure Map as a partnership, not just as a solo agent so you'll know what the specific financial goals are. Start with the end in mind, and do what's necessary to get there. If you don't know the goal, you'll never reach it.

3. Set your magic number goal based on the treasure map. Remember, that's the number of listings required to fuel your business at all times. Listings are the lifeblood of your business.

4. Set up your whiteboards as based on your goals. Create your ideal day schedule based on your goals.

5. Set up your banking so you're tracking absolutely everything in your partnership business. We recommend QuickBooks for bookkeeping and accounting, and mint.com as your financial dashboard. Remember, start with 10 per cent of each check goes into savings and 20 per cent to a tax account. Your operations account is separate and receives the net profit from each of your transactions after your costs these deductions.

6. Decide how you will market yourselves. Are you a partnership in name and brand, or only in accounting? Is one of you a listing agent and the other a buyer's agent? Are you branding yourself as a team? Know the legal requirements of your state regarding using a team name or a name other than what is on your license.

7. In order to have a life other than real estate, you must declare a starting time and a quitting time for your business day. It's not normal or admirable to work every waking hour of every day. Agents sometimes try to make this a badge of honor, but it's an indication of weak time management. A good reference for learning time management is *Getting Things Done* by David Allen.

8. Commit to running a lean, profitable, fluff-free machine. Remember, your product is profit, and profit is the result of the professional work you do for your clients and prospects. To make the profit you desire, you simply must find enough people to help.

9. Recognize that the days of "winging it" are over. Understand that you're running a business and every day you're either self-employed or self-unemployed.

10. Hire a coach. It's especially important for couples and partners to have a very interested third party to steer the ship. This helps avoid conflict between partners and couples, because all must follow the advice of their coach.

What's the income potential here? We're talking about a partnership. Just as before, this is largely determined by your time commitment, your skill level, focus and mindset. The difference with the partnership model is that now you have to not only get along with your partner, but also maintain a well- oiled, systematized machine. Using a transaction coordinator is really a requirement at this level. Using a TC generally allows the business to earn more profit, as both partners can be doing the dollar productive actions necessary to reach the goal.

It's not unheard of to produce well up to a million dollars in gross commission income under this model, but this only works when both partners are following the same plan, have sorted out responsibilities, have healthy mindsets, and are embracing the ideal day, the magic number, and the treasure map. Trying to thrive as a partnership without such direction is a recipe for disaster. The downside occurs when partners are at odds about which leads are handled in what way, and who handles more, (or less), of the workload. This in-fighting is destructive to marriages and friendships. Many coaching hours are spent in counseling of such partnerships.

Tim and I have worked together since we were high school sweethearts; we met when we were 15-16. We had a car cleaning and detailing business, so we have the advantage of having worked out the responsibilities and our strengths and weaknesses before we even got our real estate licenses. We followed Michael Gerber's recommendations made in his book *The E Myth* when we established our real estate practice, and it was one of the smartest things we did. As Gerber says, "With no clear picture of how you wish your life to be, how on earth are you going to live it?" That's why we recommend you start with the end in mind.

In his book *The Five Pillars of Getting Things Done* David Allen gives a very practical, step-by-step guide to keeping your business organized. The pillars are as follows:

PILLAR 1: Capture everything: your to-do's, your ideas, your recurring tasks. Everything. Put it in a pen-and-paper notebook, a to-do app, a planner, or any method you prefer to get organized. Whatever method you choose has to fit into the flow of your business and your life.

The barrier to using an organizing tool should be so low that there's never a reason for you to say, "I'll add it to my list later." You want to capture everything as soon as it happens so you don't have to think about it again until it's time to do it.

PILLAR 2: Clarify the things you have to do. Don't just write down a planned vacation. Break it down into actionable steps so there's no barrier to doing the task. If there's anything you can do right away, and have time to do it, then get it done. If there's anything you can delegate, do it so that those tasks don't require more time.

PILLAR 3: Organize the actionable items by category and by priority. Assign due dates where you can, and set reminders to follow-up on them. Pay attention to each item's priority. You're not yet doing any of the items on the list; you're just making sure they're in the right buckets for later. In short, this is quality time with your to-do list, your inbox and your calendar. This is the point where you decide do it, ditch it, or delegate it.

PILLAR 4: Reflect on your to-do list. Look over the to-do list to see what your next action should be. Cross things out that you know you're never going to do because they've been on your list for four or five years. Apparently, they are not important.

This is the time the clarifying step pays off. You should be able to find something that you do have the time and energy to do right away. If you see something so vague that you know you're never going to be able to pick it up and run with it, either break it down or ditch it. Give your to-do list an in-depth review periodically to see where you're making progress. We recommend a to-do list never be more than two pages long. It shouldn't be a to-do book.

PILLAR 5: Engage and actually get to work. Choose your next action and get to it. Your system is, at this point, set up to make figuring out what to do easier. Your to-dos are organized by priority, placed in categories, and filtered. You know what to work on and when to work on it. Your work is broken into manageable bite-size chunks that are easy to start. It's time to get to work.

In real estate, we recommend taking on no more than three items from those to-do lists that relate to dollar-productive activity. Your focus should be on lead-generation, lead follow-up, prequalifying, presenting, negotiating, and closing. Lather, rinse, repeat.

CHAPTER 16

Rules for the Successful Team

RULE #16: The System IS the Solution!

There are more ways than one to divide responsibilities in a successful partnership. What follows are the steps in one team model that, over the years, we've found to be profitable.

1. Identify your lead-generation spokes. Everyone has a different combination of lead-generation spokes. We recommend a combination of people you do know, such as past clients and centers of influence, plus people you don't know, such as for sale by owners and expireds, and Notice of Defaults. Identify which partner or team member will be responsible for lead-generation.

2. Identify how you will handle those incoming leads whether they are Internet leads, call-ins, referrals, and the like. The emphasis must be on urgency, so ideally one person will be in charge of incoming leads, prequalifying the leads, using buyer and seller prequalification scripts.

3. Identify who is responsible for pre-appointment work. For instance, who is sending the pre-listing package to sellers, finding homes, and setting up showings for buyers.

4. Identify who will be presenting. We do recommend to couples, depending on the partnership and the relationship, that you present together in this instance. Why? Because you'll usually be presenting to more than one decision maker, and your chances of connecting with those people are higher when you can match personality styles. Maybe you hit it off with the husband and he hits it off with the wife or vice versa. Maybe it's a probate situation, where several decision makers are involved. You want to increase your possibility of connecting with different personalities and presentation styles.

5. Decide who will handle the transaction coordination. We highly recommend that you delegate this to a professional PC or transaction coordinator. This shields you from the paperwork and funnels you into lead-generation and presentation.

6. Systematize and automate everything. Think of your transactions from beginning to end. A coach can walk you through each of these specific items. Start with lead-generation. What are your spokes? What do they cost? What are they producing? What's the system to receive them, convert, and close each lead? Commit to using scripts consistently every time in every situation.

Don't have different rules for different situations. Standardize your approach for simplicity. Memorize our rule, "The system is the solution." This way, it's not because one partner makes the rules or insists it's his or her way or the highway. It's because it's the system that's been agreed to by both partners.

The following partnership rules apply to a successful partnership and must be in place before you can even consider building a team:

1. You must have separation of responsibility. Own your jobs within the practice and be accountable for being the best at each.

Would you like a FREE copy of Tim and Julie's proven business plan?
http://FreeCoachingCallsForAgents.com

2. You must use scripts in all phases of a deal. Use your scripts consistently and they will stop sounding like scripts.

3. You must have a proven free listing package and send it prior to 100 per cent of your listing appointments. Always.

4. Follow the seven-step listing process. Use a buyer presentation in your office prior to showing homes (*see Appendix*).

5. Use a transaction coordinator.

6. You must have separate accounts for operations, taxes, and savings, and managing your money.

7. Be clear that profit is your product.

8. Follow a daily schedule which reflects your goals on both a personal and a partnership level.

9. Keep your emotions and mindset in check.

The late, real estate sales trainer guru, Howard Brinton has three great recommendations to help you keep your right mindset. First, convert anger to resolve. Anger is the biggest waste of energy on the planet. Second, don't let other people or things control your mind and your actions. It blocks your positive and creative thoughts.

Britton's third recommendation is to convert barrier to breakthrough. You may know it as an objection or even rejection, but stick to it until you win, and you will gain personal, mental dominance. He advised to take every "no" as "not yet." You don't hear only with your ears. It's an opportunity for you to learn to hear with your mind. The way you accept other's words will determine your fate. Gain an attitude of positive acceptance.

Caution, do not even consider expanding a partnership into a team if you're not following all of these rules. The team will fail if you are unclear or inconsistent with any of the critical skills we discussed.

Why even consider building a team? Profit.

There are many things to consider when building a team. Who should you hire and when? Why? What should you pay them? Who should you hire first? Again, the transaction coordinator job should be the number one hire, from the solo agent through the partnership, and certainly, for a team.

Note: Consider having all potential team members take the disc test. Take the test free at agentdisc.com.

A transaction coordinator's job lends itself to an hourly wage position. The work is performed during normal business hours, when mortgage and title companies are open. It's the easiest position to build into your team. What is the transaction coordinator's job? They take it from in-contract to close. Ideally, (this really should be a rule), they need to be licensed. Why do they need to be licensed? Because being licensed removes all questions concerning what they're allowed to do and they are not allowed to do. It removes a large amount of liability from you.

When do you get a transaction coordinator? When you're closing at least three transactions per month for 90 days straight. Do not hire one until this has been consistent. When you're considering hiring a transaction coordinator, ask yourself if you are just currently busy or if you're consistently producing at this level.

What do you pay? Usually, it's about $150 to $450 per file, depending on your market. With higher levels of production, you can consider a dedicated base pay plus fee for closing. Remember, however, if you have them on salary, they want to be paid week in and week out, whether you have a lot of closings or not. We like the per closing model, because they get paid when you get paid.

The decision to hire a buyer's agent is the next consideration. That's right. Don't hire a buyer's agent until you have a transaction coordinator. Buyer's agents absolutely must be licensed. Their job is to convert incoming buyer leads into clients. Ideally, they're also prospecting, but at a minimum they're doing lead conversion. They take buyers from leads, turn them into prospects, and then into clients. Then, once they're in contract, they'll turn them over to the transaction coordinator. Ideally, buyer's agents are not closing their own transactions, meaning, they're not doing the transaction coordinator work. That's not their job. Their job is to convert leads, show property, write contracts, and turn it over the transaction coordinator. Lather, rinse, repeat.

Buyer's agents will only convert and close what it takes them to be financially stable. You may have more leads than you have leads getting converted. The buyer's agents often will say, "Oh, the leads are no good." Or, "They're not calling me back." When in fact, they're working just to the level of what makes them happy. They're getting enough in the pipeline for them to make the income that they need. When interviewing, always ask what the buyer's agent wants before you prescribe it to them. You can't want it more than they do. Therefore, you want more than one buyer's agent, assuming you have enough lead-generation to support them.

When should you hire a buyer's agent? Only when you've achieved your magic number of listing inventory, maintained at all times, for at least 90 days straight. If you're struggling to keep listing inventory, you will struggle to maintain lead flow. Do not add to the pressure by buying leads to keep your buyer's agent happy if your listings are not already supplying that. Your listings have to do the heavy lifting to generate lead flow. Remember: You have to list to last.

How do you pay buyer's agents? We present three options for paying them:

Option A is a 25 per cent referral fee to non-team members. These are various agents. They may be in your brokerage, but they don't have to be. This is our referral fee based on a deal-by-deal basis. You can charge anywhere from a minimum of 25 percent to, in some cases, as much as 60-65 percent, depending on the situation. This is a great way to see if you like having buyer's agents without dedicating them to your team and being accountable for their financial wellbeing. In this model, you simply have to have two or three trusted agents to whom you can refer your buyer overflow. Get signed referral agreements. Track their progress and make sure you follow up. This model allows you try out different agents and hire and fire, so to speak, with greater ease, than a dedicated team buyer's agent model.

Option B is the dedicated team buyer's agent, who only works on your team. They are dependent on you. The basic model is a 50-50 split. You can certainly leave it at that for simplicity, but we base it with 15 percent going to a team leader, if they generated the lead, and 15 percent to the buyer's agent, if they generated the lead. Really, it's a 65-35 with the weight going to whoever generated the lead. This means the lead-generator gets paid back for their efforts, whether that was generated through prospecting or marketing referrals.

Option C. The position is not a buyer's agent; it's a showing agent, with a flat fee per showing. The amount per showing can vary from $10 to $25, depending on your market. They take the buyer to the team leader once the buyer falls in love with the house. They literally are just a showing agent. They're not writing contracts. They're not negotiating. They're not doing anything except opening doors. Ideally, they're searching out property so that they're showing the right things, but they're certainly not negotiating. That's why they don't make as much as a normal buyer's agent. They are less expensive, but also do less work than the traditional buyer's agent.

Now, an argument can be made that somebody non-licensed could do this job, but I think it's a disadvantage, because they can't answer questions like whether there have been price reductions, for instance, or other questions concerning money. Ideally, this person is also licensed.

Who's your next hire? After you've hired everybody else we've talked about, the next would be a listing coordinator, also referred to as a listing assistant. They do not have to be licensed. They enter new listings into the system. They take pictures, get the brochures made, the lock box, and so forth. They do basic seller follow-up and feedback. Again, ideally, they're licensed, but they don't have to be.

When do you fill the listing coordinator position? When you're maintaining 20 or more consistent listings, minimum. Otherwise, you should be able to handle it yourself or with your other staff in place. What do you pay them? Typically, a flat fee or a percent per file at closing, maybe a base salary, depending on the level of business you're cranking out. Avoiding a salary is a benefit to the team leader, since the listing coordinator would get paid his or her salary, whether you dropped three listings or whether you have 30. Again, it's nice to pay people when you're getting paid, and not to have that dependency.

A listing partner job is different from a listing coordinator. A listing partner is the next hire for your team. They do have to be licensed. What is their job? It is to convert listing leads, to go on listing appointments, and to take listings. Then to lather, rinse, repeat. We have successfully developed many teams with the listing partner or partners where they are going on listings, taking those listings, and getting them into the MLS. They're not showing buyers. They're not doing transaction coordination. They're not doing anything other than handling the listing presentation, prequalifying the seller, going on the presentation, taking the listing (ideally), and then getting it into the MLS.

Now, when do you hire someone like that? When you have enough listing leads to go on a listing appointment per day, and then usually, that person is making a percent. Depending on your situation, it could be 50-50 or something like that. Remember, all they're doing is presenting. That means the person has to be really good, because you expect him or her to be as good as you are and to take the listing.

Notice that you are never, ever, delegating the job of lead-generation, prospecting, or lead follow-up. This is the most important part of the business. Thus, it rests on your shoulders, alone. Do not live in the fantasy world thinking that you're going to delegate all of your lead-generation to some virtual assistant in the Philippines for $3 an hour. I've never seen that model work successfully. You must be responsible for your lead-generation, your prospecting, and your lead-follow up. Remember, lead-generation is the fuel for the engine of your business.

CHAPTER 17

The Master Plan to Financial Freedom

RULE #17: Rich Is Where Your Money Works For YOU!

Most people get into real estate because they have fallen in love with the Myth of the Entrepreneur. They believe the made-up fantasy that real estate will deliver to them a boss-free life, with no one telling them what to do or when to do it. They believe they can buy leads and set their lead-generation on autopilot; they can build teams with loyal minions who will do all the hard work for them, while they enjoy being "famous" from all their incredible, seemingly effortless success.

And of course, they believe they will have unlimited income and freedom where everyone is a billionaire and drives a Bugatti.

Then the hard truth settles in.

Sure, they have no boss and they control their schedules. So two out of three ain't bad, right? Yet financial success (or even financial stability) alludes them. Most agents burn out faster than a cheap flashlight at a home inspection!

So, if you started in real estate to be "rich," let's define what "rich" really means to us and the thousands of successful clients we've coached. *Rich is where your money works for you, and you no longer have to work for your money.*

That means all the living expenses you worked out in those earlier exercises are paid for every month, even if you never pick up the phone and call a FSBO ever again! Sound good?

Here is your Master Path to Financial Freedom:

Let's make a few assumptions:

- You currently owe on a home with a mortgage.

- You have some debt to pay off.

- Your desire is to be truly financially free.

- You are willing and able to stay focused for long periods of time and follow a path even when it feels daunting.

- Know that life is about base hits. Waiting for the winning lottery ticket is not your path to becoming rich.

- Know that everything worth having will take 2-3 times longer than you think it will or should.

- Know that you will be tempted to make course corrections (easy buttons) all the time. Don't.

- Know that values of your assets will go up and down and volatility will scare the pants off you.

Level ONE:

1) Become and remain a prolific earner. Make as much net income as you can, as fast as you can.

2) Be tax wise. Assume your CPA is not going to save you anything. Become literate on how to legally pay less in taxes, including the benefits of starting an LLC, S-Corp etc. Be careful who you listen to for financial advice. Ninety-nine percent of those offering

Would you like a FREE copy of Tim and Julie's proven business plan?
http://FreeCoachingCallsForAgents.com

financial advice, regardless of their title, are sales people. They are commissioned on you taking their advice. Read these books by Tony Robbins: *Money: Master the Game, and Unshakable.*

Learn about HSAs and retirement accounts that are tax free.

3) Save 10% off the top of every check, then work up to 20% off the top of every cent you earn. Put that money into an account not so easily accessible.

4) Have at least 3 months of cash on hand and work up to having 6 months of available cash to cover your core living expenses and overhead. Consider having this in a secure safe rather than a bank.

Level TWO:

Note: Dave Ramsey books are your friend.

5) Be debt free. If you have any higher interest cards, pay them off first. Psychologically, it's beneficial to pay off the cards with the lowest balances first. You will see and feel your progress.

6) Pay your house off. It's a nice way to lock in a return that you would otherwise be paying to a lender.

Level THREE

7) Now that you are debt free AND you are still earning, start buying rentals with cash. Diversify where you buy. Look for single-family homes in city centers, state capitols, and college towns. In a financial downturn, those types of markets do just fine.

Formula:

- You need $15k (or whatever) to cover all your personal overhead.
- You need $15k net from properties to make it so you are making enough net income to cover your overhead.

- You can buy homes that will pay you 8%+ net income. Take, for example, a $120,000 home in Indianapolis, Indiana. Taxes are $2k per year. Rents for $1200 per month. $1200 x 12 = $14,400 in gross rent. Deduct taxes ($2k) = $12,400 net. That's a 10% ROI.

Once you reach this level, all your income goes to buying more rentals and having fun.

Level FOUR:

8) The net income you make *just from* the rentals should be automatically invested in Vanguard Index Funds. Over time, your investments of $15k per month will make you very rich. Here's the rough math:

   If you invested $15k over 20 years, using historical averages, you would have around $9 million. Remember, this is money being invested automatically from your rentals. Your regular income can go to buying more and having fun.

9) Monitor your money every day. Use Mint or something similar to alert you. Build a dashboard for your assets and accounts. Watch like a hawk to avoid unnecessary bank fees.

This should be your short-term and a long-term "get rich" plan. If you need the income from your rentals, you could take it from the cash flow. Your worst case is mitigated because you have passive income and no debt. Additionally, your "retirement" is more than covered with your passive investing into index funds from your rental cash flow. Note: we are not tax accountants or attorneys. Consult with a trusted professional before implementing the suggestions we've given here to determine how they pertain to your personal situation.

Conclusion

We wrote this book because we recognized the frustration that real estate professionals feel. In this day of easy-button, do-it-for-you, stress-melting business solutions being offered — particularly the must-buy solutions to the "feast-and-famine" phenomenon that seems natural in the sales world — we offer a practical, tactical strategy.

In Section One, we discussed the importance of getting your mind straight; understanding, that if you are to run your business, and not the other way around, you must have a set of goals that will drive you to help the most people whom you can help, at the highest level possible. We examined the difference between a mindset of scarcity versus believing in abundance, and the impact each has on your success. We then applied these principles and showed you how to embrace new habits.

Thomas Edison said, "The successful person has the habit of doing things failures don't like to do." Focusing on real estate, Tim Harris adds that this means in order to reach ever-increasing levels of success, financial stability, happiness, and peace, you must rise to the occasion and, "Do what you don't want to do, when you don't want to do it, at the highest level."

In Section Two, we took things to the next level and discussed the most important part of your success trajectory: implementation. You learned about "spokes-on-the-wheel," and coming to terms with the fact that a strong real estate practice requires multiple lead-generation spokes. A successful practice cannot be based on just one magical, mystical solution. You learned that listings are the fuel for the engine you're running. Your "Magic Number" is the number of listings you must have at all times to meet or exceed your financial goals.

You also learned that there are only a handful of actions which lead to profit in your practice. Generating the lead, following up with urgency, prequalifying for motivation and timeframe, presenting at a high level, and using a system and closing are the filters that must strain your daily schedule.

The "Daily Success Game" is the tool we recommend to spotlight your personal accountability on that list of actions that create profit. Appointments, remember, are more important that contacts; pertaining to lead-generation, lead follow-up, prequalifying, presenting or negotiating, appointments should be the primary objective of each business day.

Taoist philosopher and reputed author of the *Tao Te Ching*, Lao Tzu, said, "An ant on the move does more than a dozing ox." This speaks of the importance of taking action daily no matter how small it may seem. We have a sign in our real estate office which reads, "Repetitious Boredom Pays Off!" Some days will seem like you're an ant on the move, other days will be overwhelming, but taking action in the first place is what matters most.

Section Three of the book covered what can result from your inspired actions taken when based on a strong mindset and well-established habits. Freedom comes from having a specific path, rather than choosing a path by happenstance. Rich is when your money works for you, and when you no longer have to work for that money. It's not your commissions that create the lifestyle of your dreams, but rather what you DO with those hard-earned commission checks.

Next, Section Three discussed if, when, and whom, one could or should hire additional team members. Different team models were examined so you can choose the path that's best for you. Remember, this business has no income cap, no stringent educational requirements, no inventory for you to purchase, and only you as your boss. This can be a curse that can cause you to squander time, money and effort, or it can be the biggest blessing of your life, if you choose to be in control.

The difference between someone who sees freedom in real estate as a blessing and not a curse is easily identified. They take action. Tony Robbins says that, "A real decision is measured by the fact that you've taken new action. If there's no action, you haven't truly tried." So, now it's decision-making time! Taking action requires movement; it stops stagnation. Even if you change courses as you get moving, it's the movement that matters. As Tim is fond of saying, "Done is better than perfect!"

It's time to stop being afraid about what could go wrong and start being excited about what could go right! It's time to take control. Begin with the end in mind and calculate exactly how many people you must help every year to meet or exceed your financial goals. Subconsciously, you'll remember the things your learned from this book and get to work, causing you to take more action sooner, and to help more people at a higher level. By reading this book, you'll have learned to do what you don't want to, when you don't want to do it, at the highest level you can. You've also learned that when you help enough people, the profit follows.

We would like to thank all of you for reading this book, for listening to our podcasts, for being great coaching clients, and for being the leaders in our industry. We know that you are the change that is occurring in real estate, that you're leading the way, instead of following blindly. We know that you're doing good work, that you're making the right decisions for yourself and your family. We are blessed to be part of your success and are your biggest fans and advocates. You're amongst friends, colleagues, and supporters when you follow what we teach. We don't want to be seen as gurus, only as practical, tactical advisors to your ever-increasing success on this planet. We hope you take this book as a guide and that it serves you well.

Appendix

The Daily Success Game

Your daily goal is to earn at least 50 points.

The accumulation of real work in real estate is what leads to consistent, predictable income. Remember, you have only 'worked' when you've scored at least 50 points each day. Each item of is worth five points.

1. Take a listing – 5 points
2. Sign a buyer to buyer agency – 5 points
3. Sell a listing – 5 points
4. Put a buyer in contract – 5 points
5. Prequalify a Seller Prospect – 5 points
6. Prequalify a Buyer Prospect – 5 points
7. Set a listing appointment – 5 points
8. Call back100% of your leads – 5 points
9. Talk to five people from your COI – 5 points
10. Talk to five Asset Managers – 5 points
11. Get a Short Sale Approval – 5 points
12. Complete five BPOs–5 points
13. Attend a COI event and add five new COI contacts to your database – 5 points
14. Talk to five expired listings – 5 points
15. Talk to five. FSBOs – 5 points

16. Send a referral with signed referral docs – 5 points

17. Receive a referral with signed referral forms – 5 points

18. Hold a homebuying or selling seminar or webinar-5 points

19. Get a price reduction of 5% or more on one of your listings – 5 points

20. Listen to the Tim and Julie Harris Daily Motivational Message – 5 points

Remember, your goal is to earn 50 points each and every day.

Let's get rolling with an example. You sell one of your listings – 5 points. The same day you prequalify a new buyer – 5 points. The buyer signs an agency contract (5 more points). You've got 15 points so far!

18 Relentless Lead Follow Up Rules

1. Relentless lead follow up means that the goal is to feel like you might be 'over' communicating with prospects.

2. BE the one who follows up, don't give up so easily like most other agents do.

3. Schedule your relentless lead follow up daily, no excuses!

4. Keep all of your leads in ONE place, using ONE system.

5. Enter ALL of your new leads into your dedicated system daily.

6. Leads are labeled either "A, B or C" quality.

7. DO leave messages when you follow up!

8. Stop believing that they will 'call when they're ready.'

9. Stop relying on your "drip system" to make you money.

10. Always call with the intention of setting an appointment, not to 'just check' on them.

11. Open house leads must be called the same day or evening of the open house.

12. Sign calls and Interactive Voice Response (IVR or 800#) calls are to be immediately called, within 5 minutes or less.

13. Internet leads must be called within 15 minutes of receiving the lead on your phone.

14. Direct referrals must be called within 15 minutes of receiving them.

15. Consider using an app on your phone or an audio recorder of some sort to keep track of leads on the go, but don't forget to transfer them after!

16. All leads must be contacted (a real conversation, not email) a minimum of three times for prequalifying, making a presentation or for more information to move them forward. If no appointment set after that, throw the lead away.

17. Realize that it takes MORE leads than you think to close the amount of deals you require.

18. Don't delegate your relentless lead follow up to your assistant – its your #1 job in real estate!

Lead Followup Conversation Starters

Fact: Most agents don't follow up like they should because they don't know what to say. Learn how to move the conversation forward so you can set more appointments in less time!

Follow Up Conversation Starters that Lead to Appointments

a) Do you still have to buy a home?

b) Do you still have to sell a home?

c) What questions do you have for me before we get started? (Looking/Listing)

d) What should we have discussed about your situation that we haven' t yet?

e) What happens if the house doesn't sell?

f) What happens if you don' t buy?

g) Is keeping the home an option for you?

h) Ideally, what happens next regarding your housing situation?

i) Tell me more about your situation.

j) Tell me more about what's motivating you to want to make a move.

k) How much time will you need before you'll be ready to move forward?

l) What help do you need from me so you' ll be more comfortable?

Then remember to A B C – Always Be Closing

The correct way to close for an appointment is to reiterate what their needs are, followed by, **"I have 2p m tomorrow available, or 10am Saturd ay, which is best for you?"**

Whiteboard Accountability & Dream Board Examples

This is a creative twist our coaching clients, Jen Teske & Jean Lewis took on Whiteboard Accountability. Rather than using dry-erase markers on multiple whiteboards, they avoid the hassle of bad handwriting and smudges, when they developed their magnetic and movable design!

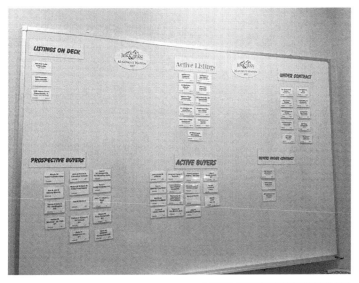

One of our long time coaching clients developed this effective ad for creating inventory. Use it as an actual advertisement or print out hard copies for mailers or to post on high-traffic community boards.

Example of a Dream Board from our coaching clients, Lance & Karen Kenmore.

Made in the USA
San Bernardino, CA
29 August 2018